FROM THE BES
THINK A

NAPOLEON HILL'S
SUCCESS
PRINCIPLES
REDISCOVERED

FOREWORD BY JEFFREY GITOMER

AN OFFICIAL PUBLICATION OF
THE NAPOLEON HILL FOUNDATION

NAPOLEON HILL'S
SUCCESS
PRINCIPLES
REDISCOVERED

TO CLAIM YOUR ADDITIONAL FREE RESOURCES PLEASE VISIT
SOUNDWISDOM.COM/NAPHILL

SOUND WISDOM
P.O. Box 310
Shippensburg, PA 17257-0310

For more information on publishing and distribution rights, call 717-530-2122 or e-mail info@soundwisdom.com

Quantity Sales. Special discounts are available on quantity purchases by corporations, associations, and others. For details, contact the Sales Department at Sound Wisdom.

International rights inquiries please contact The Napoleon Hill Foundation at 276-328-6700 or email NapoleonHill@uvawise.edu

Reach us on the Internet: www.soundwisdom.com.

ISBN TP: 978-1-937879-74-7
ISBN Ebook: 978-1-937879-75-4

For Worldwide Distribution, Printed in the U.S.A.
Previous version published as ISBN: 978-0-9830008-2-2

With contemporary commentary by Judith Williamson, Director, Napoleon Hill World Learning Center

1 2 3 4 5 6 7 8 9 / 21 20 19 18 17

Cover/Jacket designer Eileen Rockwell

*Dedicated to all the readers of and contributors to
the weekly "Napoleon Hill Yesterday and Today" e-zine.*

FOREWORD

I owe my positive attitude to Napoleon Hill. During a one-year daily four-hour intensive sales and positive attitude training back in 1972, I was fortunate enough to be exposed to Hill's principles of success.

Each day one of the eight guys on my team had to give a book report on one of the chapters in *Think and Grow Rich*. Since there were only 15 chapters in the book, we reviewed it in its entirety every 3 weeks. We went through the book more than 15 times in one year. I felt like I had memorized it.

And somewhere during that year, something clicked. I realized that by adopting the fundamental Hill principles, and adapting them to my life and family, I could achieve and maintain a positive mental attitude. I became an achiever and a believer — and have never lost that belief.

I identified with Hill's philosophy. It became part of the fabric of my thoughts, my outlook on life, and my expressions to others — both written and verbal.

Who do you identify with?

What do you identify with?

Whose principles do you follow?

How dedicated are you to achieving and maintaining a positive attitude?

Four years ago, I began an informal partnership with the Napoleon Hill Foundation to create and produce their weekly email newsletter, and was introduced to Judy Williamson. We titled the e-zine, "Napoleon Hill Yesterday and Today." Each week Judy would contribute a column that was a combination of Napoleon Hill's thoughts and teachings, combined with her insights and interpretations.

Judy Williamson is Director of the Napoleon Hill World Learning Center at Purdue University Calumet. She has been both a student and a teacher of Napoleon Hill's principles for more than two decades. Her insight is remarkable, and her ability to bring Hill's timeless success principles into the 21st century is one-of-a-kind.

This book is also one-of-a-kind.

Judy has compiled 52 lessons from Hill's writings and created challenges for you to apply and master each one. If you read this book correctly, it will take you one year to complete. It's designed to give you one lesson on attitude, success, and life each week—and you are challenged to put it into practice before going on to the next.

Napoleon Hill's success principles are timeless, and there's a reason. Actually there are a dozen reasons—and all of them create an atmosphere and environment conducive to learning, and succeeding:

1. He's gentle, and his words are gentle.
2. He's insightful, and his principles are sound and time-tested.
3. He's easy to read, understand, and apply.
4. He's on target with what's wrong and what's weak.
5. He's on target with how to make it right and strong.
6. His wisdom is right on the money.
7. His ethics ring true and genuine.
8. He reinforces his advice with real-world examples.
9. He encourages you to do it.
10. He has faith that you can achieve.
11. He warns you of outside influences that will be jealous of your endeavors.
12. He has a track record that includes tens of millions of success stories.

A thousand people have come and gone claiming to be personal development gurus. All of them quote Hill and reference him as their inspiration.

He has stood the test of time, and has remained the icon of Positive Mental Attitude. No one ever says a bad word about Napoleon Hill.

If you asked people to make a list of the top five most positive books in the world, *Think and Grow Rich* would probably not top everyone's list—but I guarantee it would be somewhere on *every* list. Pretty remarkable for an 80-year-old book.

This book is a gift. You give it to yourself *first*. Become a believer by taking action, and seeing the results. *Then* begin to share the gift with others.

—Jeffrey Gitomer
Author of The Little Red Book of Selling *and*
The Little Gold Book of YES! Attitude

Chapter 1

A crisis can force one to focus and prioritize one's actions like one has never done before. That can be the seed of an equivalent benefit that Dr. Hill was always talking about when he talked about the good that can come out of adversity. When you have no choice, things become very simple and choices become very easy. Take the crisis in which you may find yourself and use it to your advantage.

—Elie Alperstein

All too often life throws a wrench into our ordinary existence and tests our mettle. When this happens, many people go down for the count but others are resilient and rise from the ashes to become a stronger and an improved version of their past selves. If we give all we have to give and throw away the past in anticipation of a better future, we are practicing the door closing that Dr. Hill discusses.

Door closing can be viewed as lacking compassion and ruthlessly putting yourself first, but then again it can be viewed as an evolutionary tool that at least psychologically promotes the survival of the fittest. The choice is to wallow in past regrets or failures and bring others down with you, or to suck it up and positively move forward in the only direction that promotes growth. Obviously, it is a difficult undertaking, but one that needs to be determined if a person is to advance.

I have heard the saying recently that "we remember moments, not days." I like the thought because if we place the best moments of our lives on our memory playlist, just imagine how we could color our attitude in rainbow glory! Likewise, if our memory playlist includes all the darker moments that have transpired, our dark shadows would overwhelm us.

Which playlist do you choose to have playing in your mind? Only you can decide. Memories and music are frequently connected in the human psyche as well as smells and touch. Being humans, we process information through our senses. Just consider what we can do if we program our experiences to correspond to touch, taste, and sounds that elevate our moods and attitudes. Thoughts we think, emotions we feel, habits we repeat, do lead to our character development and character determines our destiny. The journey begins with the first step. What direction will you travel in?

Born Poor? Wonderful!

Dr. Napoleon Hill

You were born poor? Wonderful! So were Abraham Lincoln, and Thomas Edison, and Andrew Carnegie, and Henry Ford.

You have something in common with the truly great!

Had you been born with a silver spoon in your mouth, you would have been deprived of the opportunity to make yourself strong and resourceful through the necessity for struggle.

For struggle—as the biologists, sociologists, philosophers, and historians know—is the prime way of life. It's nature's system of sorting out the strong from the weak, of making sure that Man, as well as the animals and plants is constantly improved. In that sense, it is the will of the Creator driving us toward perfection.

Anyone can overcome poverty through determination and faith.

Sure, the fight will be a hard one. But the rewards will be so much more appreciable.

Your attitude will have a strong bearing, however, on how hard the struggle will be. Accept it as a challenge, rather than a curse, and you find the fight much easier.

There is no obstacle that can prevent you from achieving financial success if you approach it with a positive mental attitude, with full knowledge that any stumbling block can be turned into a stepping stone to greater heights of achievement.

Is lack of education holding you back? There are night schools, adult education classes, public libraries, and correspondence courses—all available at little or no cost—that can help you win an education quickly.

Do you suffer from a physical handicap? Your city, county, and state have rehabilitation centers which will minimize the disability or impediment and help you realize your dreams of achievement.

All things are possible for the person with determination and courage.

The journey of 1,000 miles begins with but a single step.

Only you can take that first step.

Decide now, this instant, on exactly what you want to achieve. Write down the goal. Commit it to memory. Keep it always before you. Then map out step-by-step the exact course you plan to follow in making it come true. Once you have done this, you are ready to take that first step toward success.

You cannot, however, ever expect to stumble your way to a higher station in life. You must have a purpose and a plan, plus the determination to carry them to fruition.

Remember, none of us is doomed to permanent poverty.

Unless we doom ourselves.

Success Unlimited. November, 1968, pp. 61–62.

CHAPTER 2

"You are what you think." To write—you must think. When you write a letter, you crystallize your thinking on paper. Your imagination is developed by recollecting the past, analyzing the present, and perceiving the future. The more often you write, the more you take pleasure in writing. By asking questions, you, as the writer, direct the mind of the recipient into desired channels. You can make it easy for him to respond to you—thus, when he does, he becomes the writer and you the recipient.

—W. Clement Stone

Even though it's still cold and sub-zero outside, our hearts long for spring. To me, turning the page on the calendar to the next month brings hope that winter is not eternal. Just thinking about seed catalogs, Groundhog Day, Valentine's Day, and Presidents' Day makes us aware that spring cannot be far behind. So, when the wind blows and the snow flies, we need to think on these things instead. Our attitude will become more positive, more pep will be in our step, and our smiles will transform the dark days of winter into the light of springtime.

February is the month for Valentines, cards, love notes, and romantic letters. Love is in the air, and both Napoleon Hill and W. Clement Stone have written essays on the subjects of love and letter writing. Each essay is packed with good thoughts and tips for practicing the age old art of keeping in touch. Why not use W. Clement Stone's self-starter, "Do it now!" and get those valentine letters in the mail early? Who knows, you might influence someone positively in your direction and get a pleasant surprise in return. It's definitely worth the effort and it will make you immortal in the recipient's eyes and hopefully heart.

Remember, when you express yourself on paper you immortalize yourself through the printed word. Even though we die, our written words can last forever. How often do you look at a note, a signature, or a recipe penned by a loved one who has passed on and think of them fondly? Our society is one of written contracts. When something is written and signed, it means more. Give more this month, write a letter and wait for the response. You won't be disappointed.

Love: The True Emancipator of Mankind

Dr. Napoleon Hill

Love is man's greatest experience. It brings one into communication with Infinite Intelligence.

It is an outward expression of the spiritual nature of man.

When Love is combined with the spirit of romance, the world may well rejoice, for these are the potentials of the great leaders who are the profound thinkers of the world.

Love makes all mankind akin.

It clears out selfishness, greed, jealousy and envy—and makes right royal kings of the humblest of men. True greatness will never be found where loves does not abide.

The love to which I refer is the "élan vital"—the life-giving factor—the spring of action—of all the creative endeavors which have lifted mankind to the present state of refinement and culture.

It is the one factor which draws a clear line of demarcation between man and all of the creatures of the earth below him. It is the one factor which determines for every man the amount of space he shall occupy in the hearts of his fellowmen.

Love is the warp and the woof of all the riches of life. It embellishes all riches and gives them the quality of endurance, evidence of which may be revealed by cursory observation of all who have acquired material riches but have not acquired love.

The habit of Going the Extra Mile leads to the attainment of that spirit of love, for there can be no greater expression of love than that demonstrated through service rendered unselfishly for the benefit of others.

If a man be truly great he will be compassionate, sympathetic and tolerant. He will love the good and bad among all humanity. The good he will love with pride and admiration and joy. The bad he will love with pity and sorrow, for he will know, if he be truly great, that both good and bad qualities in men often are but the results of circumstances over which they have, because of their ignorance, little control.

The great minds of every age have recognized love as the eternal elixir that binds the heartwounds of mankind and makes men their brothers' keepers.

If a man is truly great, he will love all mankind!

Success Unlimited. January, 1955.

CHAPTER 3

The key for me for applied faith has to be the old adage, "actions speak louder than words." Anyone can say they have faith in any-thing, yet without applying faith for a determined outcome, faith can (and typically does) fall by the wayside.

— Ron McCullough

Applied Faith is an active state of mind through which individuals seek to establish a working relationship with Infinite Intelligence. Through applied faith minds are conditioned to receive guidance from Infinite Intelligence in the form of a plan. Dr. Hill states, "When a plan comes through to your conscious mind … accept it with appreciation and gratitude and act on it at once." You will recognize that this is the correct plan by the feeling of intense enthusiasm and inspiration that accompanies its reception. Dr. Hill also states: "Faith is Nature's elixir through the use of which Nature enables man to transmute the impulse of thought into a sky-scraper of riches or a hovel of poverty."

Stop and think for a moment how extremely powerful Applied Faith can be. Biblically, we are told that it can move mountains and fulfill our purest longings as long as our desires are accompanied by works (action). Miraculously, a person is able to condition the outcome of his or her desire by persistent suggestion to the subconscious mind. When we truly want what we desire, we think about it, meditate on it, write about it, plan for its attainment, and then actually begin to take action toward achieving it one small step at a time. This close attention to detail intensifies our focus and wakes up this sleeping giant, the genie that is the powerful force known as our subconscious mind. This subconscious mind lies dormant in too many people—perhaps the 98 percent of the population that Dr. Hill refers to as drifters.

When we accept that the power within us can do great things through us and for us, it need not be in our area of interest to ask how this will occur or attempt to figure it out. Whatever mechanism is put into motion to bring this about will work, if we get out of our way. The subconscious mind, like Aladdin's genie, is willing to grant your every wish. Once commanded to perform, it will rise to the occasion and work miracles in your behalf if you only allow it to work. By knowing positively what you want, expecting it to happen, and acting as if it has already happened, you will be surprised at the quick realization of your desire.

Once received, always express immediate gratitude for the gift from your higher power and move on to create additional richness in your life. Gratitude in advance is not a bad idea either since, by expressing gratitude for a completed project, we are signaling our subconscious mind that we have already received it.

Never overlook the obvious. If you think you can or you think you can't, you're right! Thinking makes it so. Applied Faith is the oil that keeps your magic lamp lit and your personal genie standing at attention ready to grant your every wish. Decide to be the master of your fate—do it now!

FAITH vs FEAR

Dr. Napoleon Hill

FEAR is faith in reverse gear. Fear is a negative belief in something, and belief is the very foundation of faith.

Faith is a positive mental attitude in action.

Your mental attitude is the sum total of your thoughts at any given time.

A positive mental attitude has its roots in the spiritual wells of one's soul. And it is the medium by which adversities may be transmuted into benefits.

Your achievements are limited only by your mental attitude, for it is true that your only real limitations are those which you set up in your own mind.

Keep your mental attitude RIGHT and your future will always be BRIGHT. Success goes to the person whose mental attitude is such that he expects success. And health, wealth, happiness are products of a positive mental attitude.

Your mental attitude, whether it be positive or negative, weaves into your character every thread of your thoughts.

A positive mental attitude is the factor which makes prayer pay off. Keep your mental attitude positive and everything else will take care of itself in your favor.

People who work with a positive mental attitude are constantly doing the "impossible."

The difference between mediocrity and genius is mainly a question of mental attitude. If you don't like what life has given you, change your mental attitude and attract something else more to your liking! And remember that not all of the wisdom of the sages and the ages can help the person who quits trying to help himself.

Remember that the Creator has so made us that our strength grows out of our struggles, and we are no bigger than the circumstances which we permit to frighten or worry us.

Faith is a state of mind which has been called "the mainspring of the soul," through which your aims, desires and plans may be translated into their physical equivalents.

Besides a positive mental attitude, free from negatives such as envy, hatred, jealousy and fear, applied faith has other fundamentals.

These include: A definiteness of purpose, supported by personal initiative or action ... recognition of the fact that every adversity carries with it the seed of an equivalent benefit; that temporary defeat is not failure until it has been accepted by you as such ... the habit of expressing gratitude for one's blessings daily, in the form of a prayer.

To create a mental attitude favorable for the expression of applied faith, follow these instructions:

1. Know what you want and determine what you will give in return for it.
2. When you affirm the object of your prayers, let your imagination see yourself already in possession of it.
3. Keep your mind open for guidance from within, and when you are inspired by "hunches"—take heed of them immediately, for they may bring you the answer you seek.
4. When you are overtaken by defeat, as you may be many times, remember that man's faith is often tested in many ways, and defeat may be only your testing time; therefore, accept defeat only as an inspiration for greater effort.

There is no such reality as a "blanket" faith. You must have a definite objective, purpose, or desire before you can enjoy the benefits of applied faith. Faith is guidance from within which will not bring you that which you seek, but it will show you the path by which you may go after that which you desire.

Success Unlimited. May, 1955, pp. 20–21.

CHAPTER 4

Despite these challenges, nothing keeps me down. A positive attitude has definitely helped me throughout my life. As a kid, I always said I was fine when people asked me how I was, even when I was hospitalized from a severe arthritis attack. Today I always say "amazing" when people ask me how I am doing.

— Tom Cunningham

When asked about happiness, Abraham Lincoln said, "It has been my observation that people are just about as happy as they make up their minds to be." That's both the good and the bad news.

When things in life take a turn for the worse, we may not be able to change the outcome of the event, however, we can change our way of thinking about what happened, our attitude. Victor Frankl teaches us in his classic book, *Man's Search for Meaning,* that our attitude is ultimately the only thing we can control in life.

Living with physical ailments, poverty, war, hatred, and a thousand other negativities that may well be beyond our control can sometimes be an ugly fact of life. But how we think about these "facts" determines our attitude toward them in our personal life. For example, if there is not enough food in the refrigerator to make a sizable meal for a family of four, do not complain but celebrate the fact that there is any food at all. Go a step further, and serve what is there on your best dishes as if it were a celebration meal. Finally, give thanks for the feast that is about to be eaten, and even serve it with candlelight. Changing the atmosphere, by changing your attitude can greatly change your perception.

Ever notice that when your perception changes, the very next outcome most often changes too? This is the magic of attitude! The magic of attitude is the very method by which we can always control our destiny. Change your attitude, change your life. If you think you can, or you think your can't, you're right!

Here are some excellent affirmations that W. Clement Stone used to keep his attitude on track. You might try incorporating them into your daily routine too and see what difference word power can make!

- To be happy... act happy!
- I feel healthy... I feel happy... I feel terrific!
- God is always a good God.
- Success is achieved by those who try and maintained by those who keep trying.
- Be courageous!
- With every adversity there is a seed of equivalent or greater benefit.
- What the mind of man can conceive and believe, the mind of man can achieve.
- Direct your thoughts, control your emotions, and ordain your destiny.
- Do it now!

Learn How to Live Your Own Life

Dr. Napoleon Hill

You will never find peace of mind by allowing other people to live your life for you.

Remember, the most profound truth in all the facts concerning mankind consists of the fact that the Creator of man gave him complete, unchallengeable right of preroga- tive over but one thing, his own mind. It must have been the Creator's purpose to encourage man to live his own life, to think his own thoughts, without interference from others. Otherwise man would not have been provided with such a definite system of protection over his mind.

By the simple process of exercising this profound prerogative over your own mind you may lift yourself to great heights of achievement in any field of endeavor you choose. Exercise of this prerogative is the only approach to the status known as genius. After all, a genius is simply one who has taken full possession of his own mind and directed it to objectives of his own choosing, without permitting outside influences to discourage or mislead him.

Henry Ford became a great industrialist and made himself wealthier than Croesus, not because of his superior ability or brains, but simply because he took possession of his own mind, fashioned in it a career of his own making, and kept all negative influences away from his mind until he attained his objective.

Orville and Wilbur Wright learned to live their own lives.

Their exercise of this profound prerogative gave the world its first successful flying machine, the forerunner of a method of transportation which is shortening the distance between all parts of the world and all people and making all mankind more closely akin.

Thomas A. Edison learned to live his own life, think his own thoughts. And his exercise of this privilege uncovered and revealed to mankind more useful inventions than had been revealed during the entire period of civilization up to his time. This despite the fact that Edison was thrown out of school after only three months of schooling with a pronouncement from his teacher that he had an "addled" mind and could not take schooling.

What a great pity the world has not many more such "addled" minds!

Through his adversity Edison discovered something he might never have learned from formal schooling. He learned that he had a mind which he could control and direct to any desired end. He learned that he could use the technical training of other men and successfully direct scientific research in connection with the most difficult problems without personally being schooled in any of the sciences. He learned that education does not necessarily come from schooling.

These and many more great truths he learned because he refused to accept the edict of the teacher who said he had an addled mind. He took full and complete possession of that "addled" mind, and through it revealed more of nature's secrets than had any other person.

Madame Schumann-Heink was sent as a young girl to a music teacher for a test of her voice. After he had listened to her a few minutes he said, "That is enough. Go back to your sewing machine. You may become a first class seam-stress. A singer, no!"

Remember, that was the voice of authority speaking. The teacher knew good voices from bad ones. But he did not know that a poor voice may be trained by the person who is determined to do so.

That was an appropriate place for Madame Schumann-Heink to have relinquished her right to take possession of her own mind. Instead, she became more determined than ever to sing well. At this point her exercise of the profound prerogative to take possession of her mind distinguished her from millions of others who have aspired to become singers but who became discouraged and quit because they allowed the "opinions" of others to transcend their own.

She was one of the few who learn that one can do anything within reason if he or she wishes to do it badly enough.

There is something very interesting about these people who take possession of their own minds and refuse to let others live their lives for them. They bounce back from a knockout blow as if they were rubber balls. Yes, and they use adversity as a shot in the arm instead of accepting it as a "kick in the pants." They convert defeats into stepping stones instead of accepting them as stumbling blocks.

The person who throws himself on the side of the "I can do it" impulse is the one who wins. He is the genius of industry, the Henry Ford, the Thomas A. Edison, the Andrew Carnegie, the Wilbur or Orville Wright.

The person who throws himself on the side of the "I cannot do it" impulse is the individual who makes up the vast majority of mankind—the type that gets a mere living but nothing more and experiences only misery, disappointment and failure throughout life.

At the end of World War I, a young soldier came to see me about securing a job. At the very outset he announced, "All I seek is a meal-ticket, a place to sleep and enough to eat."

The look in his eyes—a sort of glassy stare—told me that hope was dead. Here was a man willing to settle with life for a meal-ticket when I well knew that if he could be made to undergo a change of mental attitude he would set as his goal a king's ransom and perhaps obtain it.

Something inside me prompted me to ask, "How would you like to become a multi-millionaire? Why settle for a meal-ticket when you can easily settle for millions?"

"Please do not try to be funny with me," he exclaimed. "I am hungry and need a meal-ticket."

"No," I replied, "I am not trying to be funny. I am serious. You can make millions if you are willing to use the assets you now have.

"What do you mean, ASSETS?" he queried.

"Why, a positive mind," I answered. "Now let us take inventory and find out what concrete assets you possess in the way of ability, experience, etc. We will move from there."

By questioning, I discovered that this young soldier had been a Fuller Brush salesman before he went into the army—also, that during the war he had done considerable "K.P." duty and had learned to cook rather well.

In other words, his total assets consisted of the fact that he could cook food and he could sell. In the ordinary walks of life neither cooking nor selling would carry a man into the multi-millionaire class, but this soldier was taken out of the "ordinary" walks of life by the process of introducing him to his own mind and causing him to take possession of that mind.

Remember, this young man was not only already afloat on the ocean of despair, but he was going down for the third time. He needed not only a lifebelt, but he needed also a stimulant to enable him to recover from the shock of misery and want he had just experienced. Salvaging a man who is willing to settle with life for a meal-ticket is not an easy job.

During the two hours I had been talking with this young man my own mind had been at work. My mind was positive. It was not weakened by hunger and hopelessness. It was a success conscious mind.

Taking the two assets which the young soldier possessed—the ability to sell and the ability to cook—I tried to help him assemble a plan by which he might convert them into his fortune.

"How about using your selling ability to induce house-wives to invite their neighbors in for a home-cooked dinner?" I asked. "Prepare that dinner with special cookware, and after the dinner is served take orders for complete sets of the cookware. You should be able to induce half of the ladies present to purchase."

"Very well," my young soldier friend replied, "but where am I to sleep, and what am I to eat while I am doing the work, not to mention the question of where I am to get the money to purchase the necessary cookware?"

Isn't it strange how the mind jumps to all the negatives and sums up all the obstacles in one's way when the mind is negative?

"Let me worry about all that," I replied. "Your job is to get yourself in the frame of mind of wanting to become a multi-millionaire by selling cookware."

While the young man was getting started in his new venture, I gave him the use of our guest room and his meals.

He also had the use of my charge account to buy some new clothes. I went on his security for the purchase of his first outfit of cooking utensils.

That was all he needed. He was in business. During his first week he cleared nearly $100 on the sale of aluminum cookware. The second week he doubled that amount. Then he began to train other men and women whom he managed in the sale of cookware under the same plan.

At the end of the first four years he had made a little over $4,000,000. Moreover, he had set into motion a new selling plan which is now netting many millions of dollars annually to men and women who sell by the same plan that he established.

When the ties that bind a human mind are broken and a man is introduced to himself—the real self that has no limitations—I fancy that the gates of hell shake with fear and the bells of heaven ring with joy!

Success Unlimited. June, 1956, pp. 9–13.

Chapter 5

All human beings have a dominant communication trait. The four basic traits are the "Driver," the "Inspirational," the "Supportive," and the "Cautious" personalities. The four DISC styles apply to all races, genders, and nationalities. Based on these one-word descriptions, would you say are you a D, I, S, or C?

— Fred Wikkeling

What type of person are you? Do you enjoy the limelight or do you prefer to be working behind the scenes? Are you a "doer" or a "thinker" or both? Do you communicate best by words or by action? Research has shown that the more you understand yourself, the better you understand others. With this in mind, Dr. Hill created a personality inventory that allows students of success to assess their personal traits and characteristics. If you visit us at www.naphill.org you can take this test online and get immediate feedback as to your score.

Tools such as this success profile provide us the opportunity to stand back and objectively evaluate our success traits. The more we know about our motives, the more we can control our motivation and our subsequent habits that we consciously or unconsciously form.

Likewise, the more we learn about our inner workings, the more in tune we are to the behavior of others. Since nobody seeking success works in isolation, it is a good idea to learn what makes others perform as well. When we learn to enhance productive beliefs and attitudes, we expand our success performance level.

Certified instructor Fred Wikkeling believes that positive visualizations and using the DISC method for discovering our own and others' personalities, enables him to be the super salesman he is in his life's work. By seeing himself successful and by understanding the hidden motivation behind people's personalities, Fred is able to bridge the gap that allows him to connect to the customer and close the sale. As a certified instructor, Fred eagerly shares this method with anyone who wants to learn, and he assures his students that if they follow his two-step approach, they will improve their success rate overwhelmingly.

Fred teaches that the DISC method will enable you to quickly ascertain a person's world view, and then approach them at their level of understanding, not yours. This intimacy not only creates camaraderie, but also allows you the opportunity to see "where that person is coming from." Next, you can then create an alliance based upon your newly acquired information that will allow you to make a positive connection with this person. By noticing the thought mechanisms that they use, you will be able to "connect" on their level by appealing to their personality style.

Dr. Hill has found that personal magnetism and body language go hand in hand. Words have been found to be the least significant part of a verbal message. Rather, facial expressions, tone of voice, enthusiasm and body language give out more signals about the "real" message than the words themselves do. It seems that when our spirits open up to the message we intend to deliver, words do not hold the meaning, but rather our method of delivery does. As listeners and/or observers of someone communicating, we need to be aware of this seeming contradiction. The quotation, "Your actions speak so loudly that I can't hear what you are saying," rings true here. Knowing this, we not only need be aware of what we say, but more importantly how we say it.

Use the success profile questionnaire, visualization, and Fred's DISC system to learn all you can about the inner workings and motives behind your actions as well as the actions of others. You will improve your success score immensely by using these techniques.

The Capacity to Understand People

Dr. Napoleon Hill

The man who is rich in the understanding of people always recognizes that all people are fundamentally alike, in that they have evolved from the same stem: that all human activities are inspired by one or more of the nine basic motives of life, viz:

- The emotion of love
- The emotion of sex
- The desire for material gain
- The desire for self-preservation
- The desire for freedom of body and mind
- The desire for self-expression
- The desire for perpetuation of life after death
- The emotion of anger
- The emotion of fear

And the man who would understand others must first understand himself.

The capacity to understand others eliminates many of the common causes of friction among men. It is the foundation of all friendship. It is the basis of all harmony and cooperation among men. It is the fundamental of major importance in all leadership which calls for friendly cooperation. And some believe that it is an approach of major importance to the understanding of the Creator of all things.

The Master Key to Riches. Fawcett Crest Books, 1965, p. 23.

CHAPTER 6

To ensure that one is receiving the whole, undiluted, bona fide truth, no matter what the subject—seek it from as close to the original source as possible. Accept no less than the real thing, and always have the courage to ask questions.

—Jeanne R. Berry

E verybody knows that it is difficult to overcome temptation. The promise of fame, fortune, and success for little work on our part seems too good to be true. Generally, it is. Success without work lacks the substance that is satisfying. When things are handed to us, we do not appreciate them as much as if we earned them. You know this to be a fact if you follow anyone's life who has inherited wealth or a title. The personal ties that connect a person to their achievement are non-existent when something has been simply "gifted" to them.

Think back to the achievements that you value the most. I remember several in my life that I like to relive though my memories, and each one involved much work on my part. If the prize was just handed to me without my effort, it would have been a hollow victory because my heart and soul would not have been in it. I guess simply put, what you earn, you value.

Many people believe that they can ride on another's coattails to success. These hangers-on view this as a shortcut to avoiding their own hard work. By self-admission, Napoleon Hill states that he spent over twenty years on his research for the *Law of Success*. He knew that two decades was a lengthy time to pursue his goal of uncovering the "secrets" that made entrepreneurial men of his day successful, but he also knew that it was like mining for gold—it would require him to exchange his time for the achievement of his desired outcome. As a consequence, he unlocked the door today for many individuals who can read and capitalize upon his research and then take it to the next level in their own lives. For this and more, followers of Napoleon Hill are grateful.

As you begin to create your own success empire, be unique, be yourself, but be anything but a copycat! I always remind myself to go to the source of the material, not the secondary information. Secondary information is about the source, but not the source. If you want to find out what's in a classic for certain, you must read the classic itself.

Be careful that you don't get all fired up about "new and improved," "never before published," "just released," and "what they didn't want you to know," because more often than not you have just been cheated out of learning from the true source of information. Remember, if it appears to be too good to be true, it probably is. Use your personal insight to weed out the "get rich quick schemes," and use the only time tested and true way to get rich—through your own thought coupled with persistent and continuous action.

If you are interested in which books are endorsed by the Napoleon Hill Foundation, visit our website at www.naphill.org and read the column written by Robert Johnson. He clarifies how you can identify a Foundation-authorized work. It is worth the little time it will take you to read this because then you can be certain that what you purchase does return royalties to the Foundation begun by Dr. Hill. Think accurately and you can be sure to judge our books by their cover because they will always have the Foundation's crest visible in plain view.

How To Hurdle Temptation

Dr. Napoleon Hill

Here's a sure-fire method to help you live the life you want to live.

To develop a positive mental attitude, you must make a habit of transmuting every experience into definite action, promptly and decisively.

That means you must have a definite philosophy, a clear-cut general standard of behavior, to guide your thoughts and actions under various circumstances.

The most important rule you can make for yourself is this: never, under any condition, engage in any transaction which does not bring equal benefits to all persons it affects.

Remember that for one person to gain, it is not necessary for someone else to lose. The only true measure of success is whether everyone concerned is benefited by it.

The late Cyrus H. K. Curtis, founder of the *Saturday Evening Post*, defined success as "the ability to get everything one desires or needs without violating the rights of others."

Through such standards of positive thinking and performance, you can achieve material success honestly, forthrightly and proudly. Let me give an example of how Curtis himself put this philosophy into action.

In the early days of the *Post*, the business frequently was short of operating capital. But Curtis had decreed that he would not accept certain types of advertising.

One Saturday, he and his son-in-law, Edward Bok, were opening mail with the hope enough money would come in to take care of the payroll later in the day. Suddenly Bok whooped: "Here it is! Enough for twice what we need!"

Curtis looked at the check in the envelope and said, "Sorry, we can't accept it." It was from an advertising agency which, learning the *Post* was pinched, seized the opportunity to try to induce Curtis to run copy he had often rejected as objectionable.

"We will operate the *Post* without this sort of advertising," he said, "and the time will come when this policy will pay off."

And another time, when heavy debts threatened to crush the *Post* out of existence, Curtis' biggest creditor—a paper company—not only extended his credit but loaned him enough money to satisfy the other creditors. Thus

Curtis was given a free hand to get his publication on a going basis.

Many years later, another firm solicited Curtis' business by offering a lower price. Curtis rejected the offer. The company that stood by him in his day of need, he said, would count on his business in his day of prosperity—regardless of price!

You will find your own decision easier to make if you have established certain standards of moral performance to which you adhere rigidly under all conditions.

In a sense, you are making decisions in advance—before you actually need to make them. For you are rejecting certain courses of action as repugnant or unworthy.

Thus you will find frequently, when a decision must be made, that it is one you made years ago when you resolved to live up to certain standards of behavior.

Remember, that you can compromise with others—but not with yourself.

Success Unlimited. May, 1968, pp. 37-38.

CHAPTER 7

Being able to think from the inside out, rather than from the outside in, enables us to block out external distractions that can impede our performance, such as environment and economic conditions, and instead allows us to tap into the infinite potential within our own mind.

– Charles Mulraine

lbert Hubbard wrote the remarkable little essay entitled, "A Message to Garcia" and it was published well over a century ago in March, 1899. The story details the personal initiative of a soldier who is assigned a difficult mission. The essay's theme is "get the job done" however you have to do it. Today, the message is still applicable. Too often when an assignment is made, the receiver stalls while questioning the details. This not only prevents the assignment from being accomplished, but removes the opportunity of success for the receiver. This could be what regrets are made of—not accepting your unique mission that only you can accomplish in this lifetime.

I have often considered a quote that says something like "God would not give you the desire if you did not possess the talent to fulfill this desire." God or Infinite Intelligence provides the necessary components for each of us to succeed at a goal, mission, or definite major purpose that we decide is our definite chief aim in life, but He does not walk the path for us. That is what we have to do.

Consider what your "Message to Garcia" might be in your life. Is it a higher education degree, is it an opportunity to be of service to a community, is it business success, or is it the richness of family and friends? Whatever your desire, if you accept the challenge with a "can-do" attitude, you will surely achieve it, because someone higher up felt you were capable of the mission. If you challenge it, disregard it, ask for an easier detail, or decline it, you will never know what you might have become if you just put unnecessary delay aside and met the task head on! Next time you are confronted with this choice, do it now, and see how proud you will be with the accomplishment that was yours for the taking.

You have probably heard the quote, "God is in the details," too. Well, maybe your "detail" is your homework assignment on this planet. Why not get about following your divine orders and see what lesson you learn? You never know until you accept the mission. The only question God might ask us on judgment day is, "Have you carried out your orders?"

Dependability

Dr. Napoleon Hill

Among the many qualities necessary for you to advance is that "old-fashioned" one called Dependability. John D. Rockefeller, Sr., once told me he rated dependability as the most important trait he looked for in selecting people for responsible positions.

On one occasion, he said, he made a trip abroad and instructed one of his trusted lieutenants to make a certain investment at a fixed time.

While Rockefeller was away, however, market conditions changed. Instead of carrying out instructions, the employee invested in an entirely different security and the transaction paid off several thousand dollars more than if Rockefeller's directions had been followed.

But his action didn't bring the employee the reward he expected. Instead, Rockefeller reprimanded him.

"Dependability means that one can be depended upon to carry out instructions to the letter," he said. "In this one instance, your arbitrary action worked out all right.

"But it could have been disastrous. Next time, get in touch with me before making such a decision yourself."

There is an old saying that there are three parts to issuing an order. The first is to issue the order. The second is to make sure it is carried out. The third is to make sure it is carried out right.

Under the system of shipbuilding developed by Henry J. Kaiser during World War II, dependability was the prime consideration. Parts, equipment and men had to be at the right place at the right time to maintain production schedules.

Consequently, he hired many expediters to keep production flowing—and ran frequent personal double checks himself to prevent bottlenecks. Once, for example, he needed several carloads of special materials in a hurry and warned a key worker to keep the train rolling to its destination at all costs.

"If any trainman looks like he's going to delay the shipment, get the president of the railroad on the telephone, if necessary, and tell him why it must arrive on time," Kaiser said, "and if he doesn't cooperate, let me know and I'll go to the government itself."

The man who knows the value of dependability in his associates, and refuses to settle for anything less than perfection, is bound to be a success.

Elbert Hubbard, the writer, placed such store on dependability that when Felix Shay applied for a position with him, he gave Shay a unique test. Hubbard instructed Shay to go to the stable, saddle a horse, and lead him around the barn 100 times for exercise. Shay did it with question.

Then Hubbard directed Shay to write a 1,000-word essay on the life and habits of the honey bee. Again Shay did what he was told without question.

As a result, Shay become one of Hubbard's most trusted associates and remained with him until Hubbard died in the *Titanic* disaster.

There is no substitute for dependability.

Notice that the word "depend" comes before "ability" in spelling the word.

Many executives rate the two qualities that same order in choosing employees for advancement to high positions.

Success Unlimited. July, 1967, pp. 33–34.

CHAPTER 8

Often times, continued support and nurturing of an employee will in the end yield a much stronger and more reliable individual. Just like my red wegilia, one employee may bloom quickly but be unable to sustain that level over an extended period.

— *Gordon J. H. Newman*

Remember... the creation of habits requires repetition through physical action.

— *Napoleon Hill*

Have you ever really considered the nature of giving? I mean true giving that emanates from your inner self without the expectation of a corresponding return? This type of giving over time becomes a habit that can be immediately manifested to change your life. When you give from surplus, it is a hollow gift. However, when you give from your present allotment, the gift takes on a magnified meaning. I am not speaking about monetary gifts here, but rather the gift that comes from the internal you—your spiritual and emotional self.

Consider for a moment the gift of time. Each of us has the same seconds, minutes, and hours in a day. Some people are able to budget this time and create a "surplus" amount to give away in assistance to others. Most people decline the opportunity to make a gift of their time stating that "when time is available," or "when I find the time," or even, "when I retire I will have the time," as criteria for freely giving this gift. Unless we withdraw the time from our own day now and invest it in others, we will never have a return on this deposit. Later is too late.

Consider also the gift of assistance. Have you been asked to help someone with a task or a project that you could easily do because you have the essential knowledge and experience? What is easy for you might be difficult for someone else. If we "gift" our knowledge and experience to someone with the idea of showing them how, not only do we contribute through our action but pass on our knowledge as well. This type of gift earns double bonus points.

Consider too the idea of changing your habits toward giving. Dr. Napoleon Hill talks about Cosmic Habitforce as being the Comptroller of the Universe. When we recognize this law and understand that as a microcosm of the macrocosm, whatever habits we put in place in our lives create our ultimate destiny. Therefore, it makes good sense to be magnanimous in the creation of our self-made habits. This is true because as we expand in our world view, our habits must expand with us if we are to flourish rather than diminish in the space we occupy in the here and now.

Fereric Amiel states, "For the conduct of life, habits are more important than maxims because a habit is a maxim verified. To take a new set of maxims for one's guide is not more than to change the title of a book, but to change one's habits is to change one's life. Life is only a tissue of habits." Consider this as a point well taken and begin right now to change personal habits wherein you want to add richness to your life. Leave money out of the equation for now. Give gifts of time, experience, knowledge, self, and notice how your new habits create a positive change in your life. Doors will open to you where none were apparent before! Try it and see!

Cosmic Habitforce

Dr. Napoleon Hill

Here you have a most profound principle; in fact, the master principle through which all natural phenomena are expressed; the power through which all the sciences are relentlessly carried out with invariable certainty; the principle which perpetuates the species of every living thing, causing each to adapt itself to its environment; the principle which fixes the thought habits of man so definitely that man is ruled by his habits.

There are only three principles underlying the voluntary establishment of a habit. They are very important, so remember them well:

1. Plasticity, which is simply the property or capability of changing or being changed. It also implies that once a change has been made, the new form established remains until a subsequent change modifies it. In other words, plasticity is the sort of flexibility found in a piece of modeling clay used by children in school. It may be molded into any desired shape and it will remain in that shape until it is molded into a different shape. Man, of all living creatures, is the only one who possesses this characteristic of being plastic, of being capable of change, and his plasticity lies, of course, in his mental faculties. Man may be changed by external influences or his environment; or he may voluntarily change himself, by exercise of his will power. This prerogative obviously is a basic necessity for the formation of voluntary habits.

2. Frequency of impression. As we have seen, repetition is the mother of memory. It is also the mother of habits. One of the factors affecting the speed with which a habit can be established is how often the action or thought involved is repeated. This, of course, varies with the individual, the circumstances, and the element of time. A thought can be repeated only so many times a day, for instance, and if a man is at work, circumstances may prevent his thinking of the particular habit he wishes to establish. There is also the matter of personal

initiative. A man may be lazy and indifferent, or he may be ambitious and energetic. This will affect the number of times he will repeat the action or thought. This, in turn, affects the length of time it will take him to establish the habit.

3. Intensity of impression. Here is another variable in the process of establishing a habit pattern. All through these principles you have been told of the importance of a strong, compelling motive, and a burning desire, as essentials. Here is the reason. If an idea is impressed upon the mind, backed with all the emotion you are capable of, it will become an obsessional desire. Thus it will have a greater impact than if you simply express an idle wish, even though the words you employ are identical. The degree of intensity of impression is, therefore, another factor which affects the speed with which a habit may be developed and set.

PMA Science of Success. Pp. 507–508.

CHAPTER 9

What do you believe? In your car called Life are you a driver or a passenger? Are you awake or snoozing? Are you speeding down the road wildly and recklessly, perhaps endangering you fellow passengers? Have you pulled off to the side, lost, looking for directions? Are you about to run out of gas? Whatever you see in your mind's eye is a reflection of what you believe. If you think you're the driver or if you think you're the passenger, just remember ... you're right!
— John Cramer

You've heard the saying, "Hope springs eternal," I am certain, but do you really believe it? Many times people are hopeless and find little reason to believe in the imaginary, pie-in-the-sky, end of the rainbow, optimistic outcomes that we are told to focus on time and time again. What do you look forward to when you are down-in-the dumps, feeling like pond scum and classified by others as one of the bottom feeders in life? What then can make you find hope when hope has left the building?

Last Saturday I gave a talk to an international teachers' organization entitled, "Getting Back to Basics — Maintaining a Positive Attitude." Close to 100 current and retired teachers were in the audience. In considering the topic, I decided to recall the outstanding moments of my teaching career because these were the moments that gave me the incentive to continue in the profession. These moments were not when I reached tenure or the top of the pay scale or even when I received a good evaluation or an award, but rather occasions when I touched the future for an individual student.

These moments did not occur daily or even weekly, but when they did they helped define my career and caused me to focus on creating other such moments for students. I remember one situation in particular. A student, Mike, was known as a quarrelsome student who failed the junior level required English class twice before he enrolled in my do-or-die summer school class. I was told by his counselor, his former teachers, and by anyone who had an opinion that Mike was trouble in capital letters. I decided that I needed the summer employment so Mike and I would have to tolerate each other for the duration of summer school. Ultimately, Mike became one of my best students, and passed the class with a high grade—but this is not the end of the story.

One day, going through the lunch line at school, I was talking about Mike to my assistant and stated that Mike proved himself very capable, was a strong student, and had a great deal going for him despite what others said to the contrary. When I arrived at the cashier, she looked at me and said only "Thank you." I asked, "For what? I haven't paid you yet." She responded, "You're the first teacher in eleven years of school who has ever said anything positive about my son." Not only was I taken aback, because I did not know that this was Mike's mother, I was hurt because this child had to wait eleven years for one positive remark from a teacher. Think about it. Isn't everybody deserving of being told they do something—anything—well? To this day, I still have the coffee cup displaying the positive affirmation that Mike's mom presented me with the next day—it begins with, "Today is a new beginning."

Today give someone a positive remark, a verbal pat on the back, and see what a difference you can make just by saying something sincere and positive. Get back to the basics of what it means to be human—acknowledge someone for their contribution and make a difference now where it ultimately counts the most.

An Approach to Faith

Dr. Napoleon Hill

Here is a story which we would like to pass on to you. A man was driving from Los Angeles to Palm Springs, rolling along just fine—until his car stopped dead. He tried the starter repeatedly, but not a cylinder would fire. Being a business man and no mechanic, he didn't know the first thing about the mechanics of his car. But he got out, lifted the hood and looked in rapt amazement at the confusing array of gadgets which greeted his eyes. Angered by his own mechanical ignorance, he slammed down the hood, locked the car and started down the highway to find a garage.

For nearly three miles he trudged along in the hot desert sun and arrived at a garage in a good sweat. The mechanic drove him back to his stalled car. Now when the mechanic lifted the hood, he knew what to look for, and he loosened a nut on the side of the carburetor, took out a tiny screen, held it up to the sunlight and, after a glance, blew on it quickly. He shook it a few times and put it back in. The engine immediately responded to the starter. All that was wrong with the engine, the mechanic explained, was that the flow of its gasoline had been temporarily shut off by the dust which had collected on the little screen. Being somewhat of a philosopher, the mechanic made the observation that men are like that sometimes—their mental screens become clogged and they fail to accept the bounteous blessings with which a generous Providence has surrounded them.

That caused the driver to do some thinking. He had received a tremendous lesson in applied faith. Suddenly he realized how many unhappy situations in life are caused by interruptions of inflowing life-energy from Infinite Intelligence. He understood more clearly than ever before how the screen of the mind, clogged by doubt, fear and worry, could shut off the life-giving inspiration and energy which is forever flowing around us.

This simple story brings us face to face with the matter of applied faith.

We feel keenly the responsibility that we have assumed in attempting in lay before you a practicable, working technique for taking possession of the forces of the universe in which we live. We will do our best to tell you what faith really is and explain the source of its power. Here is a simple method by which you may make faith effective in your life. When you understand applied faith, you will have taken a long step forward toward achieving your objectives.

PMA Science of Success. Pp. 81–82.

Chapter 10

Too often in our own lives we forget to celebrate the small successes which are the stepping-stones for greater things to come. Take time to nurture your dreams and speak life to them on a daily basis. If you forget to water them they will shrink back or maybe even die. It is vital that we all learn the power of speaking words of love and of life over every situation in our lives. Every word you speak has power.

— Loretta Levin

Spring is here. Life is renewing, grass is greening, skies are bluing, flowers are sprouting, birds are winging, trees are leafing, and the soil is warming. I wrote the last sentence because it has been stated that God is a verb not a noun. As we see the evidence of Infinite Intelligence at work in our world, we are amazed at all the intricate manifestations of the magnificence of the Universe. How can a person not be in awe when a tulip blossoms or the first robin warbles its cheery morning song? The grandeur is remarkable. Sometimes, we just need to sit and take it all in. I love the quote by Emerson that states, "The earth laughs in flowers." Can you imagine anything more wonderful than springtime after a barren, cold, and dark winter season? If we could "see" hope, I am certain that hope would look like springtime in the Midwest as Easter egg colors dot the countryside with their vibrant hues. Yellows, pinks, reds, greens and even whites cause one to stop and enjoy the beauty of it all. It is remarkable.

Wouldn't it be wonderful if we could internalize this renaissance, this feeling of jubilation and force feed our inner selves with this awesome demonstration of God's goodness? I think we can. By stopping to observe and really see what is happening about us, we can only conclude that if Infinite Intelligence cares for nature in this demonstration of yearly renewal, it cares for us equally or even more so. Springtime puts a lilt in our step, cheeriness in our laughter, and even a reason to greet the day as a new beginning.

I think that we can begin new practices to acknowledge the passage from the dead of winter to the rebirth of spring. Shedding winter coats, driving easily on dry pavement, and walking sure footed without slipping on ice or snow all make this season seem like we have released a heavy load. Why not release some old thoughts, worn emotions, and feelings that have festered over time? A good practice can be to buy some economical black balloons and blow them up, then go outdoors and release them to the Universe. Saying goodbye to things that hold us back can have a very strong therapeutic effect. Likewise, focusing on good intentions can be represented by gold balloons that we release to carry our wishes, desires and goals to a higher ground. If you are an eco-friendly person and choose not to release balloons, why not write your negative and positive releases on small slips of paper and then burn them and allow the smoke to ascend like incense to the heavens? It serves the same purpose. Or you can buy a jar of bubbles from the dollar store, and go outdoors and blow bubbles envisioning your cares or goals floating up to a Higher Power.

Whatever you decide to do as a ritual, create some rites of spring that serve as passages to a new beginning for yourself. Spring cleaning isn't just for your house. It's for your interior home too.

Some Habits Fixed by Cosmic Habitforce

Dr. Napoleon Hill

The heavens declare the glory of God; and the firmament sheweth His handiwork (Psalm 19, v. 1) sang David, the inspired psalmist. And indeed the heavens are one of the most obvious and most awesome testimonies to the presence and power of this law of cosmic habitforce.

The stars and planets operate with clocklike precision. They never collide, never get off their appointed course, but roll on eternally, as the result of a preconceived plan. Infinite Intelligence is behind that plan. If anyone doubts the existence of Infinite Intelligence, that person need only study the stars and planets, and the precision with which they are related to one another, to become convinced of Its existence.

Another outstanding marvel of creation is the human mind, which is capable of projecting itself into the heavens and predicting astronomical occurrences to the moment, many years in advance of the actual event.

Back of this there must be order. Nature and the universe are organized and ordered. This order, or reliability, of nature simplifies life. It is not necessary to understand all of the laws and order of the universe to make them effective in our lives. They operate whether or not they are known or understood.

But where there is order, there is predictable action and reaction. This is what we term cosmic habitforce. You can find the fundamental principles by which you can relate yourself favorably to the forces of the universe in these lessons. The same law which holds our earth in its orbit and relates it to all other planets in their orbits, both in time and space, relates human beings to one another in exact conformity with the nature of their own thoughts.

Time, space, energy, matter and intelligence are nature's building blocks with which she creates all things.

Another striking illustration of cosmic habitforce is found in the seasons of the year. We know without doubt that we are going to have spring, summer, fall and winter in that order. They do not always occur in the same intensity, but they do come and go, year in and year out because the law of cosmic habitforce is arranging and controlling them.

PMA Science of Success. Pp. 489–490.

CHAPTER 11

Having an attitude that is positive or negative affects more than just you. It affects your work, customers, clients, co-workers, and everyone you come in contact with.

—Mac McGee

Words represent a social aspect of who we are. They are form-fitting to our attitudes and breathe life into our desires. If only we were able to fully understand the dynamics of words, we would be well on the path to attaining our life's purpose. As we verbalize our mental imagery we are really only a few short steps away from manifesting what it is that we want to have happen in our lives.

Napoleon Hill teaches us that, "… every thought you release comes back greatly multiplied, to bless or curse you." He cautions us to watch our thoughts and to be certain that we consciously only send out and receive positive ones. Thoughts are transformed into words when we verbalize our desires. Negative thoughts, words, and actions are highly contagious and can rub off on someone a little at a time. They are like hitchhikers that we allow to ride in our car, and before we know it, these same hitchhikers have moved into our home. All because we let our guard down, and allow negativity to enter our personal space. Fortunately, the reverse can be true as well. Good words fertilize good attitudes.

Words can give us an attitude of control when we practice using them with consideration and caution. Our conscious mind uses words to create our reality and our subconscious mind uses affirmations to increase our frequency of thoughts. With these two techniques combined, our subconscious mind then connects with our waking mind and also with the mind of Infinite Intelligence. This continuum of thought blends inspiration and practice. Together these two ingredients promote intelligent action that can lead to the realization of our greatest desires.

Consider your words and how you use them today. In speaking, research indicates that words hold only 7 percent of the total meaning. Tone and body language add the huge remaining percentages. Sometimes, many times, it is both what you say and how you say it that creates the result. Be positive and learn to customize your verbal and non-verbal communication for your greatest potential reward.

The Spoken Word

Dr. Napoleon Hill

Believe in the power of the spoken words and see to it that you speak no word which does not harmonize in every respect with your positive mental attitude. An essay by Dr. S. L. Katzoff will aid you in recognizing the importance of the spoken word.

The greatest mischief maker is the human tongue. It is not what we say that counts, but how and when.

Tactfulness will never dethrone the ego from its pedestal.

Measure your words with the yardstick of courtesy, sentiment and gratitude.

Conversational interest is based upon making another feel important, and replacing telling with asking.

The less we say, the less we may have to take back. Nature knew her business when she gave us two ears and only one mouth. An unbridled tongue even one word thoughtlessly spoken may destroy the happiness of a lifetime.

To prevent fault finding and bickering, invite criticism, give merited praise, quickly admit guilt, and do not hesitate to say, "I'm sorry." Settle disputes as quickly as possible. Every moment of delay adds coals to the fires of dissension.

Finally, a reference table on successful conversation:

· Adopt a face to face method.
· Do not interrupt.
· Be responsible.
· Modulate the voice.
· Omit unfavorable references to the past.
· Give advice only when it is requested.
· Avoid negative comparisons.
· Applaud what you like and ignore what you don't.
· Never argue over unimportant details, for if you win, you will have gained no advantage.
· Guard your words and your words will guard you.

PMA Science of Success. Pp. 231–232.

CHAPTER 12

The life we all live in front of our children is analogous to a mirror; it will reflect integrity and honesty if that's what we see looking into it.

— Ernest Lehti

Impatience is not a virtue. It can even become a vice if a person allows it to overtake good, practical sense. It takes time for maturation to occur, and in most instances it does not happen overnight. Trying to force an outcome is like trying to remove a butterfly prematurely from the cocoon. When you intervene and prevent the butterfly from strengthening its wings during its struggle for release, you deny it the right to mature according to nature's plan.

Why is it when we are told to "wait and see" our impatience often gets the best of us? We react when we should have simply waited and allowed time to work its magic. Trying to manipulate the "desired" effect when we have already put the "cause" in motion is as silly as stealing the butterfly from its home. Things take time to come to fruition. Nature takes her course in the external world, and the internal world is no different. We must patiently wait and anticipate, really expect a positive outcome apply faith until inevitably truth prevails.

Sometimes what appears to be success is only a masquerade. If success is taken from someone else before their success develops into full bloom, the robber deserves no praise or adulation. There is no satisfaction in delivering a thing you did not create or put into effect. Be certain when judging a person's credibility that you ask Napoleon Hill's fact-finding question, "How do you know?" The answer you receive will enable you to separate fact from fiction, and even an impostor from the real thing.

43

People who rob others of their rightful property never really earn it. They only steal it for a time, and then in due course it finds its way back home and rests with its rightful owner. The cause always produces the effect. What goes around comes around. Feel the tug of universal consciousness at your very core, and ultimately know that you can't fool anyone—not even yourself—for very long. Truth prevails, so be on the side of universal truth and you will always walk on the sunny side of your life.

Every Act Rewards Itself

Dr. Napoleon Hill

"Every act rewards itself." That is Emerson speaking. We shall visit with him soon. You realize, I am sure, that the reward of any act may not be a "reward" as such, but rather a penalty if that is what the act deserves. The act rewards itself, not you in the sense that is meant here, and so the "reward" is fitting.

This, you may say, is nothing but old-fashioned morality. Indeed it is. It is modern morality as well, valid when man invented the wheel, valid when, perhaps, man will invent the means to duplicate himself in a test tube. And it is more than morality. I have shown you the Law of Compensation at work in my life in the hope that you will stop and think of ways it has worked for you. You will see these ways as manifestations of cause and effect. You performed some action and that "got the ball rolling." But can it be an accident that thousands of years of commentary refer to the fact that the act of giving invariably precedes the act of receiving? That when we "cast bread upon the waters" it does come back?

We see the Law of Compensation as it brings us a better job, a sum of money, an opportunity to fulfill ourselves, a meeting with someone who turns out to be a lifelong

---

partner in love and there is much we do not see. Unseen, silent forces influence us constantly. Some are good for us, some are harmful. This volume speaks on many pages of the solid, bread-and-butter aspects of life; but it speaks as well of the unseen and the omnipresent. As I show you how to be rich with peace of mind I also show you how to choose the friendly, invisible forces rather than the unfriendly, and how to make the favourable forces your allies.

Now let us sit down with Mr. Emerson by candlelight in his book-lined study:

> Every act regards itself, or, in other words, integrates itself in a two-fold manner first in the thing, or in real nature; and secondly, in the circumstance, or in apparent nature. Men call the circumstance the retribution. The casual retribution in the circumstance is seen by the understanding; it is inseparable from the thing, but is often spread over a long time, and so does not become distinct until after many years. The specific stripes may follow later after the offense, but they follow because they accompany it. Crime and punishment grow out of one stem. Punishment is a fruit that unsuspected ripens within the flower of pleasure which concealed it. Cause and effect, means and ends, seed and fruit, cannot be severed; for the effect already blooms in the cause, the end pre-exists in the means, the fruit in the seed.

"There is a third silent party to all our bargains." Remember that! The Sage of Concord continues:

> Men suffer all their life long, under the foolish superstition that they can be cheated. But it is as impossible for a man to be cheated by anyone but himself, as for a thing to be, and not to be, at the same time. There is a third silent party to

all our bargains. The nature and soul of things takes on itself the guaranty of the fulfillment of every contract, so that honest service cannot come to loss. If you serve an ungrateful master, serve him the more. Put God in your debt. Every stroke shall be repaid. The longer the payment is withholden, the better for you; for compound interest on compound interest is the rate and usage of this exchequer.

Grow Rich With Peace of Mind. Ballantine Books, 1967, pp. 143–144.

Chapter 13

It wasn't until I was in medical school that two mentors introduced me to Think and Grow Rich. Within its pages, many of the principles I was already using were validated and many others were discovered.

— Daniel Williams, M.D.

How large a part does intuition play in your life? When you have a feeling that something is brewing in relationship to your life, do you heed or reject the insight? Oftentimes, signs precede events in our lives and if we document these signs we won't be astonished when the event shows up. For example, you might experience a feeling of anticipation, a sense of foreboding, or just an edgy sensation that implies something is about to happen. Either you can acknowledge the feeling and wait for the outcome, or you can shake it off and say you were just being superstitious, that the Universe does not communicate with you in advance in this fashion. But, in the back of your mind there is that still small voice that is nudging you to listen and take note. How can a person be certain if the message is real?

A technique that I use to document this flash of advance awareness is journaling. When I feel something is tapping me on the shoulder, speaking to me in my dreams, or sending me physical signs that are meaningful to me, I jot down the date and the occurrence. I may even add a sentence or a phrase as to what this potentially could mean to me in the here and now. After a few weeks pass or maybe a month, I go back and review my entries. By then, it is easy to see if a pattern develops or if my imagination was simply running away with me. Both things can occur. In order to discern the difference, putting down what is occurring in writing establishes a pattern, a record, that it is credible and proves or disproves a person's extra sensory perception in real time.

Why not begin today and keep a log that documents when the Universe tickles you or even offers you a soft kiss on the cheek? These little intrusions in your daily routine could be the presence of your Unseen Guides directing you to consider one path over another. Their whispers could impact your life if only you pause long enough to consider what message might be being broadcast to you. When you tune in and really adjust your dial labeled Insight, you may just find that you and the Universe are in perfect alignment.

What does all this mean? It means that you need to step up and listen to the messages that can impact your life. Napoleon Hill states that when an idea comes through to you from the Universe, don't argue, don't hesitate, don't complain, but act immediately to receive the gift that has been placed in your awareness. Not tomorrow, not later, but now. This idea could just be your ultimate Key to Success.

Unseen Guides

Dr. Napoleon Hill

After I had met with one failure after another, and each time was tempted to desert or neglect my major mission in life, I began to notice that the effects of each failure were immediately wiped out the moment I got back on the track and began to carry out my mission. This happened so often that it could not be explained away as a mere coincidence.

From personal experiences, I know there are friendly Guides available to everyone who will recognize them and accept their services. In order to avail oneself of the services of these unseen Guides, two things are necessary: first, one must express gratitude for their services; second, one must follow their guidance to the letter. Neglect in this respect will bring sure, if not always swift, disaster. Perhaps this may explain why some people meet with disasters, the cause of which they cannot understand; disasters which they do not believe to be the results of any fault on their part.

For many years I was so sensitive concerning the unseen Guides, whose presence I had felt, that I carefully avoided all references to them, in both my writings and in public lectures. Then, one day in a conversation with Elmer R. Gates, a distinguished scientist and inventor, I was overwhelmed with joy when I learned that he not only had discovered the presence of unseen Guides, but he had formed a working alliance with them which enabled him to perfect more inventions and procure more patents than had ever been granted to the great inventor, Thomas A. Edison.

From that day on I began to make inquiries of the hundreds of successful men who collaborated with me in the organization of the Science of Success, and discovered that each of them had received guidance from unknown sources, although many of them were reluctant to admit this discovery. My experience with men in the upper brackets of personal achievements has been that they prefer to accredit their success to their individual superiority.

Thomas A. Edison, Henry Ford, Luther Burbank, Andrew Carnegie, Elmer R. Gates, and Dr. Alexander Graham Bell went to great lengths in their descriptions of their experiences with unseen Guides, although some of these men did not refer to these invisible sources of aid as "guides." Dr. Bell, in particular, believed the invisible source of aid was nothing but a direct contact with Infinite Intelligence, brought about by the individual's stimulation of his own mind through a burning desire for the attainment of definite objectives.

Through the guidance of unseen forces, Madame Marie Curie was directed to the revelation of the secret and the source of supply of radium, although she did not know in advance where to begin looking for the radium, or what it would look like if she found it.

Thomas A. Edison had an interesting view as to the nature and source of the invisible forces which he used so freely in his work of research in the field of invention. He believed that all thoughts released by all people at all times are picked up and become a part of the ether, where they remain forever, just as they were released by the individuals; that anyone may tune in and contact these previously released thoughts by conditioning the mind, through definiteness and clearness of purpose, to contact any desired type of thoughts which may be related to that purpose. For example, Mr. Edison discovered that when he concentrated his thoughts upon an idea he wished to perfect, he could "tune in" and pick up from the great reservoir of the boundless ether thoughts related to that idea which had been previously released by others who had thought along the same line.

Mr. Edison called attention to the fact that water runs in course, through rivers and streams, renders a great variety of services to mankind, and returns finally to the oceans from which it came, there to become a part of the main body of water, where it is cleansed and made ready to begin its journey all over again. This coming and going of water, without diminishing or increasing its quantity, has a definite parallel in the energy of thought.

Mr. Edison believed that the energy with which we think is a projected portion of Infinite Intelligence; that this Intelligence becomes specialized into myriad ideas and concepts through the brain of man, and when thoughts are released they return, like the water returns to the oceans, to the great reservoir from whence the energy came, and are there filed and classified so that all related thoughts are arranged together.

You Can Work Your Own Miracles. Fawcett Columbine, 1971, pp. 45–47.

CHAPTER 14

Napoleon Hill got it right when he said: "Every adversity, every failure, every heartache carries with it the seed on an equal or greater benefit." With my other medical complications, my depression went undetected for 13 years. While this was unfortunate, I believe it has shaped me into the person I am today. During that time I was, for the most part, able to develop methods of coping with the condition.

– Rodwell Faulkner

At times, most of us go through bouts of depression. Depression occurs in a person's life for multiple reasons and, usually these causes relate directly or indirectly to the seven fears that Napoleon Hill mentions in his writings. These fears are: fear of poverty, criticism, ill health, loss of love, old age, loss of liberty, and death. The seven "ghosts" of fear throw us on the negative side of life and cause us to worry many times unnecessarily. Still, it is difficult to counteract these worrisome thoughts every time one or two crop up. By learning about what makes one fearful, a person can arm himself against the cumulative effect of the toll these fears can take.

Dr. Hill states that "The person seeking success must force himself to control his fear by taking the first step toward his goal."

In death and dying research, Dr. Elisabeth Kübler-Ross states that there are five stages that individuals experience in the dying process. The stages are: denial, anger, bargaining, depression, and acceptance. People intent on confronting a fear move through these very same stages since these stages mirror the change process. Knowing that there is a sequence of steps that people need to take in order to change makes the process more rational and controllable for individuals. Positive Mental Attitude

The Stages of Change
Source: Elisabeth Kübler-Ross's Stages of Death and Dying

enables each of us to retain the "I can" attitude even in the face of fear. It is the right mental attitude in all circumstances.

I like to remind my students that when they are in the depression stage that can be viewed as a positive thing since the step labeled "depression" is the last step before "acceptance." Once a person accepts the change that they are going through, the cycle is complete and transition and/or learning has occurred. The struggle has ended and the worry is over.

Consider a change that you are processing. Identify what stage you are currently in, and forecast where you need to go before the change is complete. In this manner, there is always light at the end of the tunnel!

Condition Your Mind Properly

Dr. Napoleon Hill

Remember: anything you fear will trail you around like a pet dog: poverty, ill health, criticism, loss of love. The mind attracts the physical counterpart of that on which it dwells. The majority of people going through life think of those things which they don't want, and they are getting every one of them.

Wouldn't it, therefore, be a good idea to refuse to think about the things you don't want and feed your mind with pictures of the things you do want? This is nothing more important in your entire life than learning the art of keeping your mind focused upon the things, conditions and circumstances of life which you really want. This is the greatest application of applied faith you can make. When your mind has definiteness of purpose, you are in a condition to start having faith. And when you have faith, you can call upon the vast reservoir of Infinite Intelligence to assist you in carrying out your objectives.

Have you ever wondered why prayer sometimes doesn't work? Has it occurred to you that there may be something wrong in the way you pray? Prayer always works, but not always in the way you want it to. When you go to pray with your fingers crossed, after everything else has failed, and only half believe that your prayer will be heard and answered when you approach prayer with an improper mental attitude: you will not receive the answers you want. Because the dominating thought in your mind is negative, you may be sure that Infinite Intelligence will give you a negative answer.

The art of being grateful for the blessings you already possess is of itself the most profound form of worship, and incomparable gem of prayer.

It can be truthfully said that seldom in life will you fail to accomplish an act or achieve a purpose if you condition your mind properly before you start. It all depends on the way you condition your mind.

It is a fact that man is the master of every other living thing on this earth. If we look about us we can see that the birds of the air and the beasts of the jungle have been wisely provided with food and the necessities of their existence through the Divine plan. Is man, then, not worthy of the same blessing?

54

All that you need to do to get anything you rightfully should have is to take possession of your own mind and use it. You do not have to ask anyone for this privilege. It's yours... now! The approach to liberty, freedom, good health, love and an abundance of the material things of this life is through your own mind, but the methods described in this and other lessons of the PMA Science of Success philosophy. The purpose of this philosophy is to explain how you may take possession of your own mind and use it intelligently to fulfill the measure of your creation.

PMA Science of Success. Pp. 103–104.

CHAPTER 15

Worrying is the greatest loss of energy. It is as the unharnessed power of the wind lost forever. But on the contrary, engaging our minds in an active positive meditation is like constructing many windmills and capturing the power of the wind to light up thousands of homes in rural Indiana, USA.

— Uriel "Chino" Martinez

Napoleon Hill states: "Whatever the mind can conceive and believe, the mind can achieve." Belief supreme! If you can "see" it, you can "be" it. Our subconscious mind cannot distinguish between an actual event and a vividly imagined experience. This simple truth can lead to overall improved performance if we use visualization to our advantage. It can be as simple as daydreaming with added focus and clarity. Here are some beginning steps that you can try when practicing the art of visualization:

- Give yourself a "time out" and relax in whatever position suits you. Stay mentally alert, and begin to focus your attention on being free from concerns and worries.
- Begin to see in your mind's eye something positive that you want to achieve and build a "storyboard" frame by frame as vividly as you can imagine wherein you see yourself achieving this goal.
- Use your senses to add enthusiasm and energy to your mental movie. See, hear, taste, smell, and touch your goal by adding illustrative images. As in coloring a picture, you can "color" in all the glorious Technicolor images of your success event.
- Practice over and over again by concentrating on the one image that you want to "develop." Do not rob yourself of achieving this

goal by diluting your mental imagery. Focusing on one achievement is the key.

- Conclude the movie of your mind by staying in the moment and telling yourself that this is true for you now. You are the champion of your visualization. It *is* true for you.
- Come back to your wakeful state and remind yourself to practice several times daily to further your goal—conceive it, believe it, and achieve it!

When you internalize your goal, and mentally see yourself achieving it, you will begin to structure the mental imagery with the external practices that aid you in walking your talk. Results follow when actions are taken. You first ignite the cause and then follow through with the intended result or effect. It is a cause/effect world, and by putting the thought into motion, you will sooner than later reap the result.

Is There a Limit to What Belief Can Achieve?

Dr. Napoleon Hill

Your subconscious mind is your hidden boss, then, and gives orders to your conscious. But your subconscious, as you surely know by reading this book, is a very special kind of boss. It will go into conference with you, so to speak, and consider changing any of its standing orders, canceling them, substituting others if need be.

Decide upon the belief you want, set it firmly into your subconscious mind, and your subconscious will thereafter instruct your conscious mind to "live up to" that belief.

Let your belief include the concept of achievement and your subconscious mind will discover ways and means toward that achievement which, on the strength of a mere wish, would completely escape you. You may talk of "good fortune" and "lucky breaks," but what you mean is a sharpening of all your senses toward the achievement you want a focusing of all your forces away from other matters and toward that achievement a mighty access of strength and resourcefulness a tuning in upon other minds whose aid otherwise would have escaped you and more! The best of words limp when they talk of the power of belief. Only feel your belief propelling you toward the goal of your achievement and you will know at last that an irresistible force is at your command.

Is there a limit to what belief can achieve? If there is a limit, nobody has seen that limit yet. I have mentioned often that we may at times avail ourselves of powers beyond our ordinary senses. (Not supernatural, but natural powers we are only beginning to understand.) Deep subconscious belief aids mightily in winning the aid of these unseen powers.

Once, when I was a child, I had typhoid fever the only serious illness I ever have had. I was ill for weeks without showing any sign of improvement. At length, as my father informed me years later, I lapsed into a coma. The two doctors who had come out to our farm told my father there was nothing else they could do; my end was only a few hours away.

My father walked into the forest. There he knelt down and prayed to another Doctor beyond earthly doctors. With his prayer he generated a mighty, all-embracing belief that I would recover. He remained on his knees for an hour or more, and at length a great peace came over him ... that peace of mind which is the condition in which the mind words at its mighty best. And suddenly, from nowhere, and yet beyond the slightest shadow of doubt, he knew peacefully that I was going to recover.

I do not know where my father's prayer might have been heard, nor if it was heard, nor if the mere fact of the prayer gave him the focusing and intensifying agent which is part of deep subconscious belief. But I know that when he returned to the house he found me sitting up, which had been impossible for me to do a couple of hours before. Sitting up, crying for water, and with my fever "broken" as we used to say.

Grow Rich With Peace of Mind. Fawcett Crest, 1967, pp. 179–180.

CHAPTER 16

Positive creative thought leads to action and ultimate realization,
but the real power, much more than action itself, is the thought.
Remember always: "Whatever man can conceive mentally, he can
bring into materialization."

– Claude Bristol

Maintenance of Sound Health is a success principle that cannot
be overlooked for very long. When a person fails to live a
healthy lifestyle, sooner or later the results will catch up with
him. Being "over the limit" in any area related to health such as eating,
drinking, exercising, medication, therapy, and even spirituality can lead
to an imbalance that renders a person prone to illness. Moderation in all
things is not just good advice for those who can't afford the extras, it's for
everyone wanting to create the proper proportions in their lifestyle. Too
much of a good thing is too much!

Creating a healthy lifestyle requires awareness of the composition
that maintains health. In his practical advice, Napoleon Hill "imagines"
eight princes of healthy living who look after his health consciousness.
These princes are expected to perform daily duties in a person's behalf
that oversee one's total health profile. Dr. Hill puts them on watch in
order to safeguard his lifestyle from any infringers who might be the
bearers of an illness or disease. In payment for their well-performed
duties, Dr. Hill expresses gratitude to each one nightly by stating the
positive results they have accomplished during the day. This brings his
health watch full cycle.

In reality, Hill's eight princes of sound health are comparable to
reciting affirmations meant to program the subconscious mind for
personal health and well-being. Like imaginary friends from childhood,

these princes are there for a reason. The reason is to interact with the one doing the imagining in a creative way. When we draw awareness to essential health concerns we are alerting our subconscious mind that health is what we want. Stone's mantra, "I feel healthy, I feel happy, I feel terrific!" works for this reason. Make a positive start to your day by positioning the eight princes on watch and when you honor them at night for guarding your most precious commodity, be certain to express your gratitude for the treasure that they have guarded for you. Learn to call each by name, and remember that an attitude of gratitude always has and always will continue to work wonders. To your health!

The Eight Princes

Dr. Napoleon Hill

You may call the Princes by another name if you choose. Mentors, perhaps. Or Principles. Or Counselors. Or Guardians of Good Spirit.

By whatever name, the Princes serve me through a technique that is simple and adaptable.

Every night, as the last order of the day's activities, the Princes and I have a round-table session. The major purpose is to permit me to express, and thus reinforce, my gratitude for the service they have rendered me during the day.

The conference proceeds precisely as if the Princes existed in the flesh. It is a time for meditation, review, and thanksgiving, with contact made through the power of thought.

Here you may receive your first test of your capacity to "condition" your mind for the acceptance of riches. When the shock comes, just remember what happened when Morse, and Marconi, and Edison, and the Wright Brothers first announced their perfection of new and better ways of rendering service. It will help you to stand up under the shock.

And now let us go into a session with the Princes:

GRATITUDE

Today has been beautiful.

It has provided me with health of body and mind.

It has given me food and clothing.

It has brought me another day of opportunity to be of service to others.

It has given me peace of mind and freedom from all fear.

For these blessings I am grateful to you, my Princes of Guidance. I am grateful to all of you collectively for having unraveled the tangled skein of my past life, thereby freeing my mind, my body and my soul from all causes and effects of both fear and strife.

Prince of Material Prosperity, I am grateful to you for having kept my mind attuned to the consciousness of opulence and plenty, and free from the fear of poverty and want.

Prince of Sound Physical Health, I am grateful to you for having attuned my mind to the consciousness of sound health, thereby providing the means by which every cell of my body and every physical organ is being adequately supplied with an inflow of cosmic energy sufficient unto its needs, and providing a direct contact with Infinite Intelligence which is sufficient for the distribution and application of this energy where it is required.

Prince of Peace of Mind, I am grateful to you for having kept my mind free from all inhibitions and self-imposed limitations, thereby providing my body and my mind with complete rest.

Prince of Hope, I am grateful to you for the fulfillment of today's desires, and for your promise of fulfillment of tomorrow's aims.

Prince of Faith, I am grateful to you for the guidance which you have given me; for your having inspired me to do that which has been helpful to me, and for turning me back from doing that which had it been done would have proven harmful to me. You have given power to my thoughts, momentum to my deeds, and the wisdom which has enabled me to understand the laws of Nature, and the judgment to enable me to adapt myself to them in a spirit of harmony.

Prince of Love, I am grateful to you for having inspired me to share my riches with all whom I have contacted this day; for having shown me that only that which I give away can I retain as my own. And I am grateful too for the consciousness of love with which you have endowed me for it has made life sweet and all my relationships with others pleasant.

Prince of Romance, I am grateful to you for having inspired me with the spirit of youth despite the passing of the years.

Prince of Overall Wisdom, my eternal gratitude to you for having transmuted into an enduring asset of priceless value all of my past failures, defeats, errors of judgment and of deed, all fears, mistakes, disappointments and adversities of every nature; the asset consisting of my willingness and ability to inspire others to take possession of their own minds and to use their mind-power for the attainment of the riches of life, thus providing me with the privilege of sharing all my blessings with those who are ready to receive them, and thereby enriching and multiplying my own blessings by the scope of their benefit to others.

My gratitude to you also for revealing to me the truth that no human experience need become a liability; that all experiences may be transmuted into useful service; that the power of thought is the only power over which I have complete control; that the power of thought may be translated into happiness at will; that there are no limitations to my power of thought save only those which I set up in my mind.

My greatest asset consists in my good fortune in having recognized the existence of the Eight Princes, for it is they who conditioned my mind to receive the benefits of the Twelve Riches.

The Master Key to Riches. Fawcett Crest, 1965, pp. 27–29.

CHAPTER 17

I am so blessed to have studied Dr. Napoleon Hill's 17 principles of success and I am still learning to live the philosophy daily. These last 10 years have been some of the richest parts of my life.
— Christina Chia

This past week I have studied the benefits of using essential oils, explored the spiritual gifts of walking the labyrinth, meditated to the violin and didgeridoo, been reminded why faith and hope are so important in healing, and recalled that the life we create is determined by our power to choose. Amazingly, I can conclude that what my life looks like today is a direct outcome of the choices I have consciously made. If such a thing as a magic lamp exists, it truly exists in our greatest power—the power to choose. Metaphorically, when we "rub" our lamps (consciousness) and make a wish (choice) what manifests is the result of our power to select one road over another.

In life we are offered multiple opportunities simultaneously. The road we choose paves the way to our reward or penalty. In thinking about what the consequences are of making a decision, perhaps we should dedicate a little more thought to the potential outcomes and not rush through the process. If we imagine the future in advance that is customized by our decision making, we can accelerate or alleviate positive or negative outcomes. By fast forwarding to the result we can capture a sneak preview of the ending and decide whether to save it or delete it.

"If you do what you always do, you will get what you always have got!" This saying is well worth remembering. If your choices have not produced desired outcomes, then change your choices. Accept an invitation, get out of your comfort zone, push yourself harder than you have before, and change the ordinary response to receive extraordinary results. Say "yes" when you feel like "no," accept an invitation rather than decline one, be of service instead of being served, and open up rather than close down.

The universe hates two things: a vacuum and inaction. If you resort to either, something will fill the space created by the vacuum, and there will also be a consequence to your inaction. Rather than receive something that you do not want from the universe, do not create pockets of emptiness in your life or fail to act. Instead, be alert and accept the challenges that life offers. Just around the next corner could be your greatest challenge that comes along holding hands with your greatest reward. Choose to partner with your greatest power—the power to choose.

How to Develop a Definite Major Purpose

Dr. Napoleon Hill

This procedure in the development of a Definite Major Purpose is simple, but important, viz:

1. Write out a complete, clear and definite statement of your Major Purpose in Life, sign it and commit it to memory. Then repeat it orally at least once every day, more often if practicable. Repeat it over and over, thus placing back of your purpose all of your faith in Infinite Intelligence.

2. Write out a clear, definite plan by which you intend to begin the attainment of the object of your Definite Major Purpose. In this plan state the maximum time allowed for the attainment of your purpose, and describe precisely what you intend to give in return for the realization of your purpose, remembering that there is no such reality

as something for nothing, and that everything has a price which must be paid in advance in one form or another.

3. Make your plan flexible enough to permit changes at any time you are inspired to do so. Remember that Infinite Intelligence, which operates in every atom of matter and in every living or inanimate thing, may present you with a plan far superior to any you can create. Therefore be ready at all times to recognize and adopt any superior plan that may be presented to your mind.

4. Keep your Major Purpose and your plans for attaining it strictly to yourself except insofar as you will receive additional instructions for carrying out your plan, in the description of the Master Mind Principle, which follows.

Do not make the mistake of assuming that because you may not understand these instructions the principles here described are not sound. Follow the instructions to the letter; follow them in good faith, and remember than by so doing you are duplicating the procedure of many of the greatest leaders this nation has ever produced.

The instructions call for no effort that you may not easily put forth.

They make no demands upon time or ability with which the average person may not comply.

And they are completely in harmony with the philosophy of all true religions.

Decide now what you desire from life and what you have to give in return. Decide where you are going and how you are to get there. Then make a start from where you now are to get there. Then make a start from where you now stand. Make the start with whatever means of attaining your goal that may be at hand. And you will discover that to the extent you make use of these, other and better means will reveal themselves to you.

That has been the experience of all men whom the world has recognized as successes. Most of them started with humble beginnings with little more to aid them than a passionate desire to attain a definite goal.

There is enduring magic in such a desire!

The Master Key to Riches. Fawcett Crest, 1965, pp. 41–42.

CHAPTER 18

Dr. Hill and I are a good fit—purpose, passion, enthusiasm, faith—and "Pleasing Personality." Connecting has a lot to do with smiling, being open to others' feelings and ideas, caring about and hearing others, staying loose and flexible, accepting everyone into your heart, and opening yourself so others can feel comfortable sharing themselves with you.

—*Rita Golden Gelman*

For many people one of the hardest concepts to comprehend in Dr. Hill's philosophy of success is the Law of Compensation. In the principle of Going the Extra Mile, we are taught that in order to make progress in achieving our definite major purpose in life we must give before we receive. Most often students say that this is impossible because they have not received their personal windfall, consequently that have no basis from which to give. When this detail is shared, most students shake their heads and slowly repeat the word *i-m-p-o-s-s-i-b-l-e*. Let's consider this word "impossible" a little more.

Upon receiving the gift of a dictionary, Dr. Hill immediately proceeded to take a pen knife and cut the word "impossible" out, thereby ceremoniously indicating that this word does not belong in a dictionary or in a person's success vocabulary. Think about it. When we give the word "impossible" power over us, we derail whatever it is that we are attempting to do. As if by magic, we convince ourselves that whatever we deem impossible has gotten the better of us. Now, back to the Law of Compensation.

St. Francis states that it is in giving that we receive and in pardoning that we are pardoned. Notice the sequence: first we must be a giver before we can be a receiver. It doesn't matter that our gift is not financial.

Money is oftentimes looked at as the only worthy gift. But this is erroneous. Probably our greatest gift is the gift of our personal time, not our financial resources. Both are valuable, but the gift of time is something that all the money in the world cannot purchase.

So, when you are completing your six steps to riches plan as outlined in *Think and Grow Rich* and state what you intend to give in return for the money you desire, remember the Law of Compensation and the word "impossible." Nothing is impossible if you truly desire it and work yourself up into a burning desire for its attainment. Once you convince yourself that you will have it, your mind overrides the impossibility of achieving it and delivers your desire to you right on time. But, you jumpstart the process by giving freely of your time, talents, and financial resources, if available. Do not stop the cycle by demanding that you remain on the receiving end first. No hula hoop would ever get moving around a child's waistline unless the child put it into motion. Likewise, you must move in order to create the momentum for achieving your definite major purpose.

A Sharp Contrast

Dr. Napoleon Hill

Andrew Carnegie had a story about this principle of going the extra mile which he often liked to tell. "Several years ago," he would say, "a policeman noticed a light burning at a late hour in a small machine shop on his beat in which he knew that no night work was being done. Becoming suspicious, he telephoned the owner of the shop who came down immediately, unlocked the door and cautiously crept inside with the policeman.

"When they reached the small room where the light appeared, the owner of the shop looked in and, to his amazement, found one of his employees at work at a machine. The young man quickly explained that he had been in the habit of coming to the shop at night to learn how to operate the machine and thereby make himself more useful to the employer.

"The newspapers carried the story, and I happened to read it. The newspaper article made it appear that it was all a big joke on the employer. For I contacted this young man and employed him at double the wages he had been getting in this small machine shop. Today he is head of one of our most important plant operations at a salary four times what he was getting at the machine shop, and if he keeps on as he is going and continues to exhibit the same wonderful mental attitude, he will some day have our top plant job — provided he doesn't first go into business for himself.

"There is no way to hold down people who spend their spare time preparing to render greater and better service for others. These persons go right to the top of their profession or calling as naturally as a cork rises to the top of water."

There is little one can add to a story like that. It would be like trying to gild the lily. If you are ready to grasp the secret of real success, somewhere as you study the lessons in this course, you will find it. You will grasp the significance of each of these principles, and will be on the way to the achievement of your own definite major objective.

PMA Science of Success. Pp. 139–140.

Chapter 19

*There's no doubt about it, the recession has affected every industry
in this country on some level. The travel and meetings industry has
been hit especially hard.*

— Robin Powell

This week I have had the honor of traveling to Paris, Missouri,
with my Executive Assistant and meeting with the town
superintendent and invitees for the purpose of discussing
Napoleon Hill's 1952 series of six lectures given there. For me, it was a
trip back in time as we looked over archived newspaper articles found
in the *Appeal*—the town's newspaper—stood outside the home where
Napoleon Hill stayed, and wondered as a group if anyone, anywhere has
a copy of the film made a year later in that same town entitled *A New
Sound in Paris.*

The purpose of Dr. Hill's six-week visit was to begin a Success Club
wherein businessmen and others met to discuss the 17 Principles of
Success and monitor how their lives changed for the better. Charter
members assembled for evening lectures and were instructed on the
principles by Dr. Hill himself. The town never forgot Dr. Hill's visit,
and they continue to this day to wonder what became of the film—the
interviews of those charter members who were given the opportunity
one year later to say how the philosophy of success made a difference in
their life. I promised them that I would help unravel the film's mystery
and see if I could assist in locating a copy of this missing film by putting
the word out to our readership—the Napoleon Hill followers who can
accomplish any task they put their minds to.

According to Mike Ritt, the film's producer and later executive
director of the Napoleon Hill Foundation, the film was narrated by

Earl Nightingale and copyrighted. This information is available in Hill's biography, *A Lifetime of Riches,* written by Ritt and Kirk Landers. Those are the available facts, and the 9,000 people who populate Paris, Missouri, today would like to watch the film and place it in their Historical Museum.

If you have information regarding this film, please email me at nhf@ purduecal.edu. Let's see if the Universe will conspire to help us locate a copy. Then, I can show it to our conference members this August in Virginia as we present the 17 Principles of Success to their meeting planners' group and help create an incentive to reshape the economy and their hard-hit area of specialization.

The Greatest Forces are "Intangible"

Dr. Napoleon Hill

The Depression brought the world to the very borderline of understanding of the forces which are intangible and unseen. Through the ages which have passed, man has depended too much upon his physical senses, and has limited his knowledge to physical things, which he could see, touch, weigh, and measure.

We are not entering the most marvelous of all ages — an age which will teach us something of the intangible forces of the world about us. Perhaps we shall learn, as we pass through this age, that the "other self" is more powerful than the physical self we see when we look into a mirror.

Sometimes men speak lightly of the intangibles — the things which they cannot perceive through any of their five senses, and when we hear them, it should remind us that all of us are controlled by forces which are unseen and intangible.

The whole of mankind has not the power to cope with, nor to control the intangible force wrapped up in the rolling waves of the oceans. Man has not the capacity to understand the intangible force of gravity, which keeps this little earth suspended in mid-air, and keeps man from falling from it, much less the power to control that force. Man is entirely subservient to the intangible force which comes with a thunder storm, and he is just as helpless in the presence of the intangible force of electricity—nay, he does not even know what electricity is, where it comes from, or what is its purpose!

Nor is this by any means the end of man's ignorance in connection with things unseen and intangible. He does not understand the intangible force (and intelligence) wrapped up in the soil of the earth—the force which provides him with every morsel of food he eats, every article of clothing he wears, every dollar he carries in his pocket.

Think and Grow Rich. Chapter 13.

CHAPTER 20

Our schools do a fantastic job at teaching academics and we should congratulate each and every teacher for all that they do, but it takes community and parent involvement to teach kids how to be adults.

—Eddie Kilbourne

That's a wonderful lesson! I'll bet it really works for somebody else." Have you heard these statements? Or, have you made them yourself? Dr. Hill indicates that many times students fail to receive the lesson no matter how applicable to their immediate situation because they believe they are exempt. Somehow, the message always applies to someone else, but not the person in the pew.

One size seldom fits all and it takes a bit of customizing to make an assignment work especially when it comes to a person's definite major purpose. If someone tells you what to do detail by detail then in reality it is their plan and not yours. Little wonder that it does not produce the same satisfaction as living your own life's dream. When seeking your dream, it is always good to start looking first in ordinary places.

Ever wonder how to customize that path to your life's purpose? A good place to begin is at the beginning. Think back to your earliest memories. Those days when you were playing and lost all track of time and were just in the moment. Perhaps you were dancing, drawing, acting, or just marveling at the world around you as you stargazed. These were the moments you were in the zone and were not conscious of clock time. You were doing what you enjoyed doing and relished the activity. Upon reflection we discover that something we did as a child in play directly ties in to what we were placed on this planet to accomplish in our life's work.

Take a moment now and jot down those favorite playtime activities. See if you can relate them to what you now do as an adult. I would be willing to bet that there is a strong correlation between your job satisfaction and what you enjoyed doing before you began your formal education. Remember, when you mine for gold, always begin to dig first in your own back yard. That is where your greatest treasure lies. Now, pick up the shovel ... and begin right where you are. It's often been said that your treasure is where your heart is. Know your heart's desire, and you have found your greatest treasure too.

Your Beginning

Dr. Napoleon Hill

You will come to the point, sooner or later, at which you will want to do something bigger and better than you have ever done before. When you do, you are going to be discouraged by those around you who know you best, and who will say the plan you have is foolish or beyond your power to carry out. You will find more people willing to tear you down by discouragement than you will find sympathizing with you and helping you to build your ego.

The best way to avoid such discouragement is to confide only in those who have a genuine sympathy with your cause and an understanding of your possibilities. Otherwise, keep your plans to yourself and let your actions speak. Adopt the motto *Deeds – Not Words*. It is a good motto for everyone.

It may not be in the best taste for you to overestimate your abilities, but it is better than to underestimate, and it will do less harm. If you aim at a very big achievement and attain only a moderate achievement, you will still have attained something. If you allow yourself to be held back before you even begin, you will have sold yourself short and will attain nothing.

Maybe you are a man with a big idea. You have nursed this idea for a long time. You have made an experimental model, or have worked it out on paper and refined it over a period of time until you know it will work. But you haven't really done anything about it. Perhaps the reason you haven't acted is that you lack the self-confidence sufficient to start you looking for a master mind ally to help you carry out your idea.

The thing for you to do is take hold of the principles of this philosophy and apply them to yourself. It will do you no good to read these lessons and think, "That's a wonderful lesson! I'll bet it really works for somebody else." Why not start building up your self-confidence t hrough m astery and application of these time-tested principles which have lifted others from poverty to places of eminence? The rules will work for you as well as for anyone else, but you have to take the initiative. No one else will do it for you.

When a man can manage himself, he is ready to start managing others.

You have every quality in the world that it takes to succeed if you will organize what you have according to the seventeen principles of this philosophy. To do that requires self-discipline, faith in yourself and concentration on your objective. Your success or failure is entirely a matter of how you discipline your mind.

PMA Science of Success. Pp. 277–278.

CHAPTER 21

From 1908–1928 Napoleon Hill studied the success methods of such American icons as Andrew Carnegie, Thomas Edison and Henry Ford. That body of work produced Law of Success *in 1928 and then in 1937, Hill's most famous book* Think and Grow Rich. *In these works, Hill and colleague W. Clement Stone detail 17 Principles of Success which are at the core of every success case they studied.* Think and Grow Rich *and the 17 Principles of Success have taught valuable lessons to countless individuals over the past 70 years.*

— Rich Winograd

Whenever a person who inspires greatness in others passes away there is always discussion as to what motivated that person to succeed. A moment in time is generally uncovered in their life review that demonstrates they knew how to wield the power that would create their future. This power is the power of mind.

Perhaps it was overcoming an obstacle, maturing in wisdom, or just wondering what causes some people to succeed and others to fail that captured and held their interest. It doesn't matter what caused them to seek the right answer, what matters is that they took time to consider with forethought what determines a person's future.

The Law of Cosmic Habitforce applies to each and every one of us. How we interpret and use this law directly determines our outcome in life. Being part of this world and not apart from it puts this law into operation for every single person on the planet. We reap what we sow, we get what we give, and we become what we do day in and day out. This Law simply states that we — as creatures of the Universe — are under the same rules and regulations that keep the stars in the heavens and the planets in their orbits.

When we see the divine hand in our creation, our next realization is that we are under the guidance of a universal plan. Working with this plan and not against it, determines the course of the remainder of our lives. The magic or beauty in this plan is that we ourselves do not have to become God since that position is already filled. Rather, we are here to cooperate with the divine plan that leads to our highest good. In order to do this, it is always good practice to emulate those persons we admire who came before us and left us a plan to follow.

Dr. Hill suggests that we consider individuals whom we admire and next strive to become like them in the traits that we want to acquire. When we know where we are headed, the terrain is not so rocky or rough. Given a plan and a map to follow enables us to accomplish our destiny. Discover good role models, consider their character traits, and if you would like to become like them do what they did to achieve their goals. Use the READ, RELATE, ASSIMILATE, AND APPLY formula for what it is you want in life and you will be on the road to success in no time.

The Magic Plan

Dr. Napoleon Hill

"A man cannot directly choose his circumstances, but he can choose his thoughts, and so indirectly, yet surely, shape his circumstances."

As surely as the sun rises in the East and sets in the West, here is a plan that will transform your personality into whatever you wish it to be:

Place this page on the walls of your room. Each night before you retire, relax, shut out all other thoughts and repeat the following, with firm determination to build it into your character, keeping your eyes fixed upon the picture of each character as you repeat the words which indicate the qualities you wish to build by emulating that character:

LINCOLN: As I look upon your face I definitely pledge my earnest efforts to develop in my own character those qualities of patience, tolerance and love for all humanity, the weak and the strong, friend and foe, which were your distinguishing marks. I will emulate your example by looking for the good there is in others and by developing a love for justice.

EMERSON: As I look upon your face I resolve to develop in my own character those qualities which helped you to leave your footprints on the sands of time, namely, the ability to read the handwriting of Nature, as it is written in the faces of men, in flowing brooks, in the flowers, in growing trees, in the singing birds, in the faces of little children and in the rocks of prison walls.

ELBERT HUBBARD: As I look upon your face I resolve to develop in my own character that rare ability, that was your distinguishing mark, to state my conclusions in words that vibrate with life, action and enthusiasm.

WASHINGTON: As I look upon your face I resolve to develop courage and the persistence with which to complete all that I undertake.

NAPOLEON: As I look upon your face I resolve to develop the strategic ability to lay hold of the organized forces that are available for my use, and to develop the self-confidence to master all handicaps which come my way. You shall serve as a constant reminder that the quitter never wins; that eternal vigilance and the courage to carry on in spite of every obstacle are the price of success.

_____

(Sign here)

"Dream lofty dreams, and as you dream, so shall you become. Your Vision is the promise of what you shall one day be; your Ideal is the prophecy of what you shall at last unveil."–ALLEN.

Napoleon Hill's Magazine. September, 1921, p. 24.

CHAPTER 22

One industry that has influenced my family is coal mining. Coal mining has been a great tradition in Wise County for over 150 years. Coal mining has brought more jobs, money, and people to the county. Many relatives in my family have worked in the mining industry. Most people in Southwest Virginia have been affected by coal mining in a lot of good ways.

— Dalton Mullins

Hope is elusive, invisible, intangible, and can figuratively slip through fingers as if it were quicksilver. In the abstract, hope is not able to be seen, heard, touched, tasted, or smelled. If we seek out hope it can be as elusive as a leprechaun, as invisible as thought, and as intangible as the air we breathe. Yet without it our lives have lost the capacity to endure. Where does it come from and where does it go? These are important questions to answer since without hope lives can spiral down and even end prematurely.

Hope comes from the internal optimistic belief that the best outcome will occur regardless of the circumstances. It is the lighthouse of the soul that keeps the beacon lit and pointed in our direction. It uplifts us and gives us momentum for the future. Hope enriches our lives and is one of the main ingredients for a positive mental attitude. It promotes thankfulness by causing us to recognize our daily blessings. And, it inspires us to keep on keeping on because by hoping we know that the perfect end result is right around the corner. Hope is a spiritual elixir or tonic that creates a predisposition for the development of good habits. It is a "yes" rather than a "no."

Hope leaves us when we permit pessimistic thoughts to invade our mental space and take up permanent residence. Negativity spreads quickly and forces hope out. By choosing to be depressed rather than uplifted, hope vacates the poisonous environment. Like leaves caught up in a whirlwind, hope becomes entangled in the mental storm and is whisked away. Hope leaves when the environment does not support its presence. Hope is evicted and soon fear becomes the new resident.

Our power to choose creates our outcome. By staying on the positive side of the street not only do we enlighten ourselves but spread light to others. Modeling hopefulness creates the atmosphere for miracles to occur. When hope is present, people recognize that the possibility can exist for a better end result. Why not cultivate hope? You have far less to lose than if you pursued the other option.

Hope

Dr. Napoleon Hill

"Do the thing and you shall have the power."
–Emerson

The way of success is the way of struggle!

Lincoln wrote the greatest speech ever delivered in the English language, on the back of an envelope, a few moments before it was delivered, yet the thought back of that speech was borne of hardship and struggle.

All down the road of life you will meet with obstacles, many of them. Failure will overtake you time after time, but remember that it is a part of Nature's method to place obstacles and failure in your way, as hurdles are placed before a horse that is being trained, that you may learn from these, some of the greatest of all lessons.

Every time you master failure you become stronger and better prepared to meet the next one. The moments of trial will come to you as they come to all at one time or another. Doubt and lack of faith in yourself and in your fellowmen will cast their dark shadows over you but remember that the manner in which you react under these trying negatives will indicate whether you are developing power or slipping backward.

"And this, too, will soon pass away." Nothing is permanent, therefore why permit disappointment, resentment or a keen sense of injustice to undermine your composure, because they will soon eliminate themselves.

Look back over your past and you will see that those experiences of yesterday which bore heavily on your heart at the time, and seemed to end all hope of success, passed away and left your wiser than you were before.

The whole universe is in constant state of flux. You are in a constant state of change. Evolution is removing the wounds left in your heart by disappointment. You need not go down under any difficulty if you but bear in mind that "this, too, will soon pass away."

I looked back at my heavy load of grief and worry which crowded the happiness out of my heart only yesterday, and lo! they had been transformed in to stepping stones of experience over which I had climbed higher and higher.

Napoleon Hill's Magazine. September, 1921, p. 9.

CHAPTER 23

Napoleon once got a good job working for my grandmother's af-fluent family. He wrote that he "got the job because he was his wife's husband" and "pull is pull." To his credit, he later shocked my grandmother, her family, and all of his friends when he quit that high-paying job and struck out on his own. He later wrote that the job was too easy and no challenge. He felt that "inertia" was taking hold of him, a prelude to his later thinking about "drifting."

—Dr. J. B. Hill

Whenever we apply the Golden Rule we benefit every time. Just thinking about the mandate of doing unto others as you would have others do unto you is insufficient. You must take action on this thought. Simply treating others as you would like to be treated is a good start. Taking personal initiative in small things first always opens the doorway for the big things to follow later.

Today I am at the Napoleon Hill International Convention in Kuching, Malaysia. Speakers from around the world are guests of Christina Chia, who is the organizer of this convention. A touching moment for me was at a celebration dinner on the first night when she recognized people who assisted her early on with her planning for the 2007 Convention that she also chaired and sponsored three years ago. Even though some of these people were not present, she recognized them in an affirming manner and sent the positive message of her apprecia-tion forward for all to hear. She did not have to do this—no one would have known the difference—but she knew and she wanted everyone else to know too! We are all a part of what has preceded us and what will come after us. By acknowledging the work of our ancestors from the far past or our "ancestors" from our recent past, we send out blessings that express our gratitude in the eternal now. These blesssings are like what yeast is to bread. It allows the goodness to expand and grow.

This process is a simple one, yet it puts into motion the goodness that will eventually come full circle. The actions we take determine our effects in the here and now. If we respond with negativity, negative results will follow. If someone directs negativity toward us, we have the choice as to whether to break the cycle or to continue it. When we respond with a positive action, the negative energy is dispelled and we have a chance to erase the chalkboard and write something new. That is the beauty of the power of our own choice. Do good, and good follows. Do evil and grow a garden of evil outcomes. What will you decide? I prefer flowers over weeds. Do you? Blessings from Kuching, Malaysia! May you sow goodness all the days of your life.

The Applied Golden Rule

Dr. Napoleon Hill

During these times of lack of harmony among men and nations, when the world is rocked with chaos and strife and lack of faith, what greater work could a man engage in than that of planting constructive thoughts where destructive ones grew before? You have influence with a certain number of people and if you wish to exercise that influence so it will bring you the greatest return in happiness and in fortune you will lay aside all hatred or prejudice which may have fastened itself upon you and devote every ounce of your influence to helping men see the folly of strife and struggle and destructive effort. In thus wielding your influence for good you may be sure that your efforts will return to you, like a boomerang, not to curse but to bless you and yours, for as surely as the sun rises in the east and sets in the west the world will hand you back that which you hand it. You can be a man with a grievance or a man with a message; you can be a BUILDER or a DESTROYER, but make sure of this, that you can no more tear down without in turn being torn down, than you could sow wild mustard and reap a harvest of oats.

Napoleon Hill's Magazine. November, 1921, Back Cover.

Chapter 24

In Dr. Napoleon Hill's own words, "For nearly 20 years, I sought the end of my rainbow that I might claim my pot of gold. My struggle in search of the evasive rainbow's end was ceaseless. It carried me up the mountainside of failure and down the hillsides of despair, luring me on and on in search of the phantom pot of gold.

"I was sitting before a fire one night discussing with older people the question of unrest upon the part of laboring men. One of the men who sat before that fireside with me made a comment which proved to be one of the best pieces of advice that I ever received.

"He reached over, firmly grasped me by the shoulders, looked me squarely in the eyes, and said, 'Why, you are a bright boy, and if you will give yourself an education, you will make your mark in this world.'"

—Dr. J. B. Hill

L et's reflect for a few moments on the concept of freedom. The often-used expression, "Freedom is not free!" has been heard repeatedly, but instead of just nodding our confirmation, have you really considered how this statement relates to you? What part does each of us play in the freedom that we have inherited? Is it a gift that we hoard and not pass along to others, or is it something that we pay forward?

Each and every one of us as global citizens has the responsibility to protect our own freedom as well as the freedom of others. It does not matter what status we have, how rich and famous we are, or who we know. What matters is the fact that we acknowledge the gift and become its sponsor—let's call it truth in advance.

When we deny freedom to others, ultimately we are denying it to ourselves. What we share expands, and what we hoard diminishes. Planet Earth is our physical home, but we are only leasing it for our period here. We are not landlords, but renters and the care we extend to the earth will be reflected in the condition of the planet our children and grandchildren receive.

All inhabitants have universal sacred spiritual rights, and freedom is one of the abstract rights that becomes a very concrete help or hindrance depending upon whether a person has it or not. Nobody else's freedom should infringe upon our own. Isn't it time that we accept responsibility for making certain that the earth's people receive their birthright? No individual, corporation, or nation, should exploit or trespass on another's freedom. Tread softly to make the most impact. Be certain that the size of your ego does not surpass the size of your soul. Make freedom work for others before you ask for additional helpings for yourself. Play fair.

Lest We Forget

Dr. Napoleon Hill

As we read these inspiring words of the immortal Lincoln, let us remember those qualities of patience and tolerance and justice which distinguished this beloved man of the people, and built for him an everlasting monument in the hearts of his fellow men. Let us not forget that neither lowly birth nor poverty can permanently debar from fame, the person who keeps faith with those to whom he pledges his sacred word of honor to serve.

Lincoln's Gettysburg Address

Fourscore and seven years ago our fathers brought forth upon this continent a new nation, conceived in liberty, and dedicated to the proposition that all men are created equal. Now we are engaged in a great civil war, testing whether that nation, or any nation so conceived and so dedicated, can long endure. We are met on a great battlefield of that war. We have come to dedicate a portion of that field as a final resting place for those who here gave their lives that that nation might live. It is altogether fitting and proper that we should do this. But in a larger sense we cannot dedicate, we cannot consecrate, we cannot hallow this ground. The brave men, living and dead, who struggled here, have consecrated it far above our poor power to add or detract. The world will little note, nor long remember, what we say here; but it can never forget what they did here. It is for us, the living, rather to be dedicated here to the unfinished work which they who fought here have thus far so nobly advanced. It is rather for us to be here dedicated to the great task remaining before us, that from these honored dead we take increased devotion to that cause for which they gave the last full measure of devotion; that we here highly resolve that these dead shall not have died in vain; that this nation, under God, shall have a new birth of freedom, and that government of the people, by the people, and for the people, shall not perish from the earth.

Napoleon Hill's Magazine. November, 1921, p. 2.

CHAPTER 25

What do you think about when someone says, "The Golden Rule?"
When I was growing up I thought that it was only Jesus who taught
us to "Do unto others, what you would have done unto yourselves."
But when I took a comparative religion course in college, I learned
that at least eight of the world's great religions — Christianity,
Judaism, Hinduism, Islam, Buddhism, Confucianism, Taoism,
and Zoroastrianism — all teach the Golden Rule in one form or
another.

– Karen Larsen

H ave you noticed that as we scurry through life we fail to notice
the little enchantments that mesmerized us as children?
Flickering fireflies, rotund bumblebees, glorious wildflowers,
fragrant grasses, and colorful evening sunsets? Mentally we note that we
have experienced these things before and we can yet experience them
again, but can we? For each of us there will come a time when we have
reached the end of our journey and there will be an end to our sensory
capabilities.

Napoleon Hill reminds us that we need to awaken to the opportunities that meet us each day. He often relates the story about how his
stepmother switched his thinking from a negative mental attitude to a
positive one. When his father brought his new bride home, Napoleon
was determined that no one would replace his own mother. So, he dug
in his heels and readied himself for battle, but Martha complimented
him rather than scolded him, and he was won over immediately. Instead
of being the scourge of Wise County, Napoleon began to focus on living
up to Martha's high expectation of him. She had turned the tide with
one short greeting.

As we look to this day, we need to raise our own level of expectations as to the universal gifts that are all around us. By consciously looking for the good outcome, we become co-creators of the future. We find what we look for, we receive what we expect, and we appreciate what we hold dear. Reflect on this today and see if you can't be a good-finder like Martha was, and not only compliment someone and forget it, but compliment someone and watch how they reach for their potential because you noticed their gift. If not for your guidance, the person you cultivated may never have proceeded in a positive direction.

Lest I Should Not Pass This Way Again

Dr. Napoleon Hill

"I want to give good measure running o'er,
And into angry hearts I want to pour
The answer soft that turneth wrath away;
I'm sure I shall not pass again this way."

For a great number of years I have been suspecting that no one knows very much about anything. The older I grow the more convinced I become that no man knows enough to boast about.

I know I am here. I know I had nothing to do with my coming and, that I will have but little, if anything, to do with my going.

While I am here I want to do the very best I can to be happy and to help others enjoy their short sojourn by the wayside, therefore, if I have enjoyed a measure of success I wish to tell you how I did it. Also, I wish to tell you of my failures and of their cause, as nearly as I can interpret them, that you may avoid some of the pitfalls into which I have fallen in my struggle for the light of truth and understanding.

I do not know where I am going after I leave here, nor what work shall be assigned to me, therefore I believe it just as well that I do my best to be a decent human being while I am here. This will in no way lessen my chances of finding happiness, either here or in the next vineyard where I shall labor.

Whether you are Catholic or Protestant, Jew or Gentile, I want you to know that there is one round table at which you and I can sit in conference, without the question of religion or race in any way interfering, and that table may be labeled "The Table of Brotherly Love." If we meet around this table and break bread often enough I suspect that neither of us will care what is the other's religion or race. I suspect that intolerance and hatred and greed and jealousy will not find room in our hearts if we gather around this big round table often enough, because men cannot break bread together and still be enemies.

"I want to give to others hope and faith,
I want to do all that the Master saith;
I want to live aright from day to day;
I'm sure I shall not pass again this way."
　　　　　　　　　　　　　　－Ellen H. Underwood

Napoleon Hill's Magazine. October, 1921, p. 27.

CHAPTER 26

We enrich our own lives through offering our help and services to others, as much as our lives are enriched by those who offer us their help and services. It's beautiful.

— *Kathleen Betts*

How often we are discouraged from doing what we know we are capable of doing because of negative comments and concerns from friends and family. Instead of enthusiastically stating, "You can do it!" "You're the best person for the job," "I'm glad that someone has finally recognized your talent," "That creative idea will get you places," and other pat-on-the-back comments, our "supporters" say just the opposite.

Their little negative seeds become implanted in our subconscious mind and begin to sprout seedlings of self-sabotage and disrespect for our innate positive capabilities. Insidious comments from "well-meaning" supporters begin to snake their way through our psyche until they begin to rear their ugly heads from the inside out. These alien thoughts put a strain on our self-confidence and become the outcome that we never wanted in the first place. What we thought of as our million-dollar idea now is demoted to idle mental chatter. We now ask ourselves, 'How could I ever have thought I was capable of achieving that goal?" The "I can do it" mantra is replaced with the "That's a stupid idea" affirmation and all ends in the landfill of unaccomplished goals.

With a little help from our well-meaning friends and family we become resigned to the tried and true, the ordinary, the customary, and the status quo. Thoughts that are outside the norm are labeled crazy, crackpot ideas that have no practical merit. *Who would ever support me in something so extraordinarily stupid? Why did I think this was a good idea? What was I thinking anyway?* And the self-abuse goes on and on.

Stop! You are the only person who can end the negative mental bombardment. Refuse to relinquish your personal belief in a positive outcome. Listen to the naysayers, consider their well-meaning opinions and concerns, and then proceed in the direction of your own choosing armed with the ammunition that they have provided. A known adversary is easier to conquer than an unknown one, and they have just allowed you to be forewarned of their impending attack if you decide to proceed.

Do an about-face. Walk in the direction of your belief. Have faith in the outcome. And, be assured that they won't be gaining on you because they do not have the courage of their own convictions. Rather, they will continue to stay in the negative environment that they have created because it has become their comfort zone. As bad as it is, they remain there because it is a known that they can deal with rather than an unknown that you represent.

When you affirm that your greatest power is your power to choose, you honor your inborn ability to make wise, personally empowering choices. Life is what you make it. Choose for yourself and you will be the better for it.

Know Your Own Mind, Live Your Own Life

Dr. Napoleon Hill

Somewhere along the path of life, every successful man finds out how to live his own life as he wishes to live it.

The younger you are when you discover this mighty power, the more likely you are to live successfully and happily. Yet even in later years, many make the great change—from letting others make them what they are, to making sure that they make their lives to their own liking.

The Creator gave man the prerogative of power over his own mind. It must have been the Creator's purpose to encourage man to live his own life, think his own thoughts, find his own goals and achieve them. Simply by exercising this profound prerogative you can bring abundance into your life, and with it know the greatest wealth of all, peace of mind, without which there can be no real happiness.

You live in a world filled with outside influences which impinge upon you. You are influenced by other people's acts and wishes, by law and custom, by your duties and your responsibilities. Everything you do has some effect upon others, as do their actions upon you. And yet you must find out how to live your own life, use your own mind, go on toward the dream you wish to make real and solid. Know thyself, said the ancient Greek philosophers, and this remains key advice for the man who would be in all ways wealthy. Without knowing yourself and being yourself, you cannot truly use the one Great Secret which gives you power to mold your future and make life carry you the way you want to go.

Let us then take off on our trip to Happy Valley!

Do not think of me as a back-seat driver. Rather, you are at the wheel and I merely call your attention to a trustworthy road map whereon the main highway is marked beyond questions. On your journey to riches and peace of mind, the road grows smoother and straighter as you travel.

Grow Rich! With Peace of Mind. Fawcett, 1967, pp. 9–10.

CHAPTER 27

I was also struck by your emphasis on educating rather than sell-ing. I really enjoyed that. It's a delicate balance. One I suspect that would make Napoleon Hill chuckle as we look for a way to further educate ourselves to realize our fullest potential.

— Jose A. Feliciano

Education is the key to lifelong success. No one can give it to you or buy it for you. You must have a desire for it yourself and then earn it through diligent study accompanied by hard work and ongoing effort. The acquisition of knowledge is not an end in itself, but the application of knowledge is the ultimate purpose of learning. What we do with what we know, is far more significant than what we know.

It is important to remember that education does not begin and end at the schoolhouse door. After commencement, books should not be discarded as we are officially pronounced "educated." Rather books should be cultivated as good friends, even as mastermind alliances, that directly assist us in the pursuit of our goals. When you read thought-fully you actively engage yourself in the process. There is a real receiving of knowledge as you interact with the printed page and process the information. As an active reader, you are engaged and involved in an exchange of knowledge.

Why read when you can just listen to audios or watch TV? Reading is fundamental to success because the written word functions as a store-house of knowledge, a time capsule that waits for you to open it for the value that it can provide now, tomorrow, and forever. Words are immortal. We learn about the lives of legendary figures through their words and the stories written about them. Their biographies provide us with background information upon which we can customize our own lives on purpose.

Reading develops a love of learning. Learning leads to a desire for education. Proper education can lead to the development of sound character, and sound character contributes greatly to lifelong success. The process is lengthy, but there is no substitution. Put your money on education, and the dividends will be there as long as you apply what you learn! Reading provides equal opportunity for everyone who can make sense out of the printed page. It is well worth your long term effort.

The Character of Success

Dr. Napoleon Hill

A part of this philosophy is that adversity is good for us! The person who really ought to be pitied is the one who grows up with a "silver spoon" in his mouth, with a rich dad and no responsibilities! It's a safe bet that such a person will never be a very strong competitor of the individual who has had to fight hard for every foot of ground that he or she has covered.

No, it is not wealth that makes a person — it is character, persistence and a strong determination to be of service to the world! You might as well understand now that your real success will be measured and determined by the quantity and quality of service that you render the world! There is no guesswork, no luck or chance about this. It's according to nature's own laws.

You may be wealthy, but that isn't success! You may have a splendid education, but that isn't success either. You may have wealthy parents, but neither is that success, for you must remember that wealth is an evasive thing which sometimes takes wings and flies away.

The only real, permanent and worthwhile success is represented by the character you are building!

And remember that you are building some sort of a character all the time. The chances are about ten to one that if you are devoting some of your time to self-improvement, developing self-confidence and self-control, you are building a character that will be an asset to you in years to come.

Character is built slowly, step by step. Your every thought and every act goes into it. Character is the crystallization of the things you do, the words you speak and the thoughts you think! If you think about worthwhile things, you are pretty much apt to be a worthwhile person.

You can be pretty much what you want to be if your will keep your mind on the one thing you want to be long enough. Remember, I said if you try hard enough—not if you wish hard enough.

We should never complain if success does not come easily. If it did, we might not recognize it when it arrived! I have no complaint to register against fate for taking me over the pathway of hard experience. I have no kick to register against the world for the rough manner in which it has used me. An easy time in life doesn't seem to leave the proper temper in the metal. No one wants to cash a check on the Easy-Time Bank. The world is afraid of it.

The world is waiting for men and women who are seeking the opportunity to render real service—the kind of service that lightens the burdens of our neighbors; the kind of service that makes the world a better place to live in; the kind of service that ninety-five people out of a hundred do not render because they do not understand it. Shakespeare was right when he said, "our only sin is that of ignorance."

Hill's Golden Rule Magazine, 1919. Excerpted in *Think and Grow Rich Newsletter,* July 1993, Vol. 5, No. 10, p. 7.

CHAPTER 28

"I am very happy in my work. It seems that every blessed dawn brings forth new opportunities to serve and be useful to the world. I have the opportunity to accomplish good as an editor and educator." So, Napoleon Hill thought of himself as an educator. It is gratifying for me to see that so many people believe that Napoleon Hill's life work is still worth teaching.

—Dr. J. B. Hill

Have you ever had the urge to strike back, to demand the justice that is due you? Unfortunately, we have all had this desire. If we are cut off in traffic, shortchanged at the checkout, cheated by the soft drink machine, charged extra by the airlines, forgotten on our special days, or even robbed over the Internet or in person, our anger rears its ugly head and we become determined to extract the "pound of flesh" due us. Whenever we feel used or taken advantage of, the survivor instinct seems to kick in and demand that we stand up for our rights and retaliate. Whether you are experiencing this now or in the past, the admonition to "turn the other cheek" can at first seem just plain stupid.

But, for the sake of argument, let's assume that you retaliate with kindness rather than another response. Possibly, you could receive positive feedback in return, but if not you might feel that you look the fool. And you probably do. But who does your act of kindness really serve best? Yourself. You are the greatest beneficiary of your good deeds. People mistakenly believe that first and foremost acts of kindness are done for others at your own expense. The truth is that you are the greatest beneficiary of your own good. What you think about and do, you become. Thoughts followed by action and accelerated by emotion transform us into the person who does the deed.

Think about it. As you dream about the person you want to become, you add rocket fuel to the dream by igniting your emotions and traveling to your desired destination. As you stay the course by not exploring every side road you encounter, your arrival will be right on time. If we allow ourselves the luxury of digression, then eventually our dream escapes and we can no longer reach it.

When we retaliate, we take our eyes off the prize. Make sure you know in what direction you are headed before you decide to experiment with life on the sidelines. By focusing on your very best, life's little annoyances will fall by the wayside and you can travel first class rather than in baggage.

The Law of Retaliation

Dr. Napoleon Hill

Every person with whom you come in contact is a mental mirror in which you may see a perfect reflection of your own mental attitude. I recently had an experience with my two small boys, Blair and James, which illustrated this point.

We were on our way to the park to feed the birds and squirrels. Blair had bought a bag of peanuts and James had popcorn. James took a notion to sample the peanuts. Without asking permission, he reached over and made a grab for the bag. He missed and Blair retaliated with a left jab.

I said to James: "Now, see here, son, you didn't go about getting those peanuts in the right manner. Let me show you how to get them." When I spoke, I hadn't the slightest idea what I was going to do, I only hoped that stalling would allow me time to analyze the occurrence and work out a better way than his.

Then I recalled the law of retaliation that says people will always respond in kind, even in greater measure that which is deliver to them, so I said to James: "Open your box of popcorn and offer your little brother some and see what happens."

After considerable coaxing, I persuaded him to do this. Then a remarkable thing happened, out of which I learned my greatest lesson in salesmanship. Before Blair would touch the popcorn, he insisted on pouring some of his peanuts in James's overcoat pocket. He retaliated in kind!

Out of this simple experiment with two small boys, I learned more about the art of managing than I could have learned in any other manner. None of us have advanced far beyond Blair and James as far as the operation and influence of the Law of Retaliation is concerned. We are all just grown-up children and easily influenced by this principle.

The habit of "retaliating in kind" is so universally practiced that we can properly call this habit the Law of Retaliation. If a person presents us with a gift, we never feel satisfied until we have "retaliated" with something as good or better than that which we received. If a person speaks well of us, we increase our admiration for that person, and we "retaliate" in return!

Through the principle of retaliation, we can actually convert our enemies into loyal friends. If you have an enemy whom you wish to convert into a friend, you can prove the truth of this statement if you will forget that dangerous millstone hanging around your neck which we call pride.

Make a habit of speaking to this enemy with unusual cordiality. Go out of your way to favor him in every manner possible. He may seem immovable at first, but gradually he will give way to your influence and "retaliate in kind!"

The hottest coals of fire ever heaped upon the head of one who has wronged you are the coals of human kindness.

Hill's Golden Rule Magazine. March, 1919, adapted in *Think and Grow Rich Newsletter*, March, 1994, Vol. 6, No. 3, p. 4.

CHAPTER 29

Is there, however, a goal which we all may share which may in fact lead us to the elusive goal of finding our purpose in life? I think there may be such a goal and I would like to offer it to you for your consideration. The Ultimate Achievement: To be able to say that you loved your spouse as much on the day of your death as you loved him/her on the day you became married.

— Elie Alperstein

By forming mastermind alliances our creative energies are kicked up several notches. What once seemed too difficult to undertake, with a little help and harmony from our friends becomes an eagerly anticipated task or even workload. Group energy, when positive, allows the higher level vibrations to flow freely and frequently. Napoleon Hill states, "Somewhere in the cell-structure of the brain is located an organ which receives vibrations of thought ordinarily called hunches." When involved in a working mastermind alliance, these thought vibrations are increased and heightened. Hill adds, "The master mind principle, when actively applied, has the effect of connecting the subconscious sections of the minds of the allies, and gives each member full access to the spiritual powers of all the other members."

The above is one big promise, and unless you have been involved in an effective mastermind alliance, you may even be skeptical about what Dr. Hill states as fact. When two or more minds come together in perfect harmony the universe conspires within the workings of the group to bring about miracles.

Today I received a forwarded email that stated, "I think that if this group of individuals were ever to be in a room together, there is nothing that would be impossible." I smiled as I thought to myself that this is exactly what an effective mastermind alliance is meant to do. By definition a mastermind alliance is two or more people working together in perfect harmony for a positive, common purpose. Just think what could occur if the right people were put together working for a mutual, positive, common purpose. Why, the energy would be unstoppable!

Looking to jump-start your life? Wanting to form beneficial alliances of like-minded people to work with on projects of mutual interest? Why not begin by joining our Mastermind Online group? This just might be the connection that you are waiting for to position yourself on the road to success. Or, it might just serve to point you in the right direction. You can subscribe today from our home page at http://www.naphill.org.

In the meantime, seek out those individuals who will stand with you in making your dream come true!

Truly Great Master Mind Alliances

Dr. Napoleon Hill

One of the most outstanding master mind alliances you will ever read about was that which existed between Mr. and Mrs. Henry Ford. It had its beginning in the kitchen of their home, in the days when Mr. Ford was experimenting with his first internal combustion engine. It was then that he found out the important part that a wife's love and devotion play in her husband's plans. She had a sincere interest in sustaining him through the trying period of inventing and perfecting a mechanical device in order to realize his purpose in life.

The mutual appreciation of each other, and the harmony that bound them together in the months of patient effort required to make the engine run, were to last a lifetime. Although the world heard little of Mrs. Ford, who preferred to remain inconspicuous, those who know realize that she was largely responsible for the achievements of her famous husband. It was to her that he turned in moments of crisis, for her encouraging smile, her understanding admiration, her ever-fresh hope of achievement, the comfort and care that tided him over.

Their master mind alliance, based on the definiteness of purpose of two people who were willing to work in the spirit of harmony for the fulfillment of that purpose, is an inspiration to all who would achieve greatness. It is needless to elaborate on the tremendous power which grew out of this alliance, and brought into being one of the greatest industrial empires the world has ever seen. Power was generated in the minds of two humble people who knew what they wanted to do, who rendered service on the basis of going the extra mile, and who blended all their forces and concentrated their attention on their major purposes until success was achieved.

Thomas A. Edison used this master mind principle as the basis of his entire career. He did this to bridge the gaps in his own educational background by utilizing the special skills and knowledge of his associates. In this way he created the physical invention of his great laboratory. But there was another master mind alliance which was in reality far more important to him than those involving the use of physics, chemistry, and mechanics. That was the alliance with his wife. He had the good fortune to have a wife with a sympathetic understanding of his problems. She always backed him up completely in any undertaking. No matter how late at night Mr. Edison would come home from his laboratory, she was up and ready with a cheerful greeting and an eager anticipation for the recounting of the day's activities.

Mrs. Edison's confidence and faith in her husband's ability and her sustaining love encouraged him over many tough spots and inspired him to carry on against what were sometimes almost overwhelming odds.

In these last two examples you have some very important hints. Perhaps the greatest alliance any man can ever make is with his wife. If you have complete singleness of purpose with the woman you marry, there is nothing in which you cannot succeed. If you lack this harmony in your home, you might as well face the fact that you have a few strikes against you. And this works both ways. Ladies, you must have the harmony and cooperation of your husband, to lighten the burden of your work in life. It must be a two-way arrangement.

PMA *Science of Success.* Educational Edition, pp. 66–68.

CHAPTER 30

In this book, Think and Grow Rich, *Hill discussed the Sixth Sense. Indeed, he dedicated an entire chapter to this feature. I reasoned if Hill dedicated an entire chapter to the Sixth Sense, it must be important.*

— *Dr. Thomas Brown*

S ometimes I sits and thinks, and sometimes I just sits." This often-heard quote by baseball player Satchel Paige may bring a smile to our face as we recall similar behaviors in ourselves. Hot summer days and nights are conducive to sitting on porches with a tall, cool drink and just reflecting on the state of our lives. Mulling over thoughts aided by summer scents and warm breezes predispositions us for a meditative mood that easily lapses into daydreaming. Half unconsciously, we play out the movie of our life and relive the pleasant parts and hopefully skip over those episodes that need fast forwarding. These thoughts may serve as a personal inventory as to what works in our lives and what doesn't work so well.

Dr. Hill includes accurate thinking and controlled attention as two of the principles of success that students need to cultivate in order to succeed at consistently higher levels. Before a blazing bonfire of enthusiasm can be lit, the embers of these two performance based principles must be kindled and fully ignited in our personal success characteristics. And, daydreaming that leads to meditation, and meditation that leads to visioning is a good way to begin. Before you can be it, you have to "see" it. Daydreaming lends us the capacity to step into shoes that in real life may appear too large or even cumbersome. Acorns grow into tall oak trees, eagles hatch from small eggs, and a touch of genius slumbers in every daydreamer.

I had a favorite foreign language professor named Dr. Anthony Lamb, who complained in class one day about a local elementary school boarding up windows so that the youngsters would not look outside during class and have their lesson interrupted. "Why," Dr. Lamb stated, "looking out the window and daydreaming during school was the best part of my education!" I would have to concur. When we put ourselves into the meditative state that daydreaming demands, our bodies slow down and our mind and intuition pick up. The sixth sense then has an open door opportunity to enter and share opportunities, hunches, and coincidences that we may block in normal, everyday occurrences.

Why not sit and think a spell? Better, yet, why not sit and think and grow rich? Your opportunity may just be right in your own backyard as your enter that daydream that has been waiting for you all along.

The Importance of Solitude

Dr. Napoleon Hill

I love my family and my friends. My love for them is deep and sincere. I would do anything within my power to add to their comfort and welfare... but, I also love to get away from the crowds, away from everybody and visit with myself. This may seem rather selfish, but it isn't. My mental development demands it.

I love to think, to look ahead and anticipate the experiences yet to come in my life, to figure out why I am here and what to do to fulfill my read mission in life. I love to go just a step further in imagination than I have ever gone in realization. In other words, I love to do what many call "dreaming."

Contrary to what some may believe, dreaming is not harmful. In fact, quite the reverse is true. Getting away from others to dream allows you to rise above commonplace thoughts and things.

Milton did his best work after blindness forced him to turn to solitude for realization.

Francis Scott Key wrote the "Star Spangled Banner" while being held as a prisoner of war on a British ship.

When we are with others, we must be polite and discuss with them whatever subject they may happen to bring up. When we are with ourselves, we can direct our thoughts along any line we choose and concentrate upon those thoughts, impress them upon our minds and keep them where we may get them when we want them.

This is constructive dreaming!

No one ever becomes a "doer" without first becoming a "dreamer." The architect first draws the picture of a building in his mind and then places it on paper. And so we must all see the object of our labors in our minds before we can see them in reality.

Napoleon Hill's Golden Rule Magazine. March, 1919, adapted in *Think and Grow Rich Newsletter*, April, 1994, Vol. 6, No. 4, p. 5.

CHAPTER 31

We do not volitionally create our thinking. It takes place in us. We are more or less passive recipients. We cannot change the nature of a thought or of a truth, but, we can, as it were, guide the ship by moving the helm.

— Elmer Gates

When we understand how our minds work, we can then begin to apply this understanding to improving our life's circumstances. By knowing that simultaneously faith and fear cannot co-exist in our thoughts, we then realize that we can decide to be either fearful or faithful. The choice is ours. Also, when we begin to recall occurrences in our personal history wherein we either succeeded or failed, we drag along all the corresponding memories deposited in our sub-conscious mind that trail these memories like a pack of starving wolves. And, as the story goes, we decide which memory predisposes us to our future rewards or penalties by deciding which wolf to feed.

In simple terms, we create our outcomes by the thoughts that we choose to focus on with regularity. When we notice ourselves in a downward spiral due to the negative preponderance of thoughts, we can reverse our decline by deciding to focus instead on things positive. This may sound overly optimistic, but if we make a firm decision to do it with regularity, we will notice that we have turned the tide by turning our thoughts around. Fears that are focused on become more than nightmares because they also control our waking hours and even seep into our daydreams. Fear can stop us in our tracks, but faith can open wide the path that needs to be traveled. By being faithful, we cannot be fearful.

I remember a story from the parenting course that I used to teach. It went something like this:

A mother was encouraging her little boy to step outside the front door and bring in the milk that was delivered earlier by the milkman. But, it was dark outside, and the little boy was frightened by the lack of daylight. His mother, trying to reason with him, said: "Tim, don't be afraid, God is out there watching and you will be safe." Not convinced, Tim responds, "Well, if God is out there, have him bring in the milk!"

We chuckle at the story, but yet we are often guilty of the same response. Instead of boldly stepping across the threshold to get the milk, we wait and see what will happen if we don't. Soon we learn that fears can only be conquered by doing the thing we fear the most. There is no substitute for our own action. Success is not experienced vicariously, but in real time—our real time. So, step on board the success train, and face the fear that holds you back. You can only be your very best if you refuse to accept whatever is metaphorically holding you back. Don't ask someone to do what you are not capable of doing yourself. Rather, step outside the door and bring home the milk!

Applied Psychology

Dr. Napoleon Hill

The human mind is an intricate affair. One of its characteristics is the fact that all impressions that reach the subconscious portion of the mind are recorded in groups which harmonize and which are apparently closely related. When one of these impressions is called into the conscious mind, there is a tendency to recall all of the others with it.

One single act or word that causes a feeling of doubt to arise in a person's mind is sufficient to call into his conscious mind all of the experiences which caused him or her to be doubtful. Through the law of association, all similar emotions, experiences or sense impressions which reach the mind are recorded together so that the recalling of one has a tendency to bring out the others.

Just as a small pebble will, when thrown in to the water, start a chain of ripples that will multiply rapidly, the subconscious mind has a tendency to bring into conscious-ness all of the associated or closely related emotions or sense impressions which it has stored when one of them is aroused. To arouse a feeling of doubt in a person's mind has a tendency to bring to the surface every doubt-building experience that person ever had.

That is why successful salespeople endeavor to keep away from subjects that may arouse the buyer's "chain of doubt impressions." The able salesperson has long since learned that to "knock" a competitor may result in bringing to the buyer's conscious mind certain negative emotions which may make it impossible for the salesper-son to neutralize.

The principle applies to and controls every emotion and every sense impression that is lodged in the human mind. Take the feeling of fear, for example. The moment we permit one single emotion that is related to fear to reach the conscious mind, it brings with it all of its unsavory relations. A feeling of courage cannot claim the attention of our conscious mind while a feeling of fear is there. One must supplant the other. They cannot become roommates because they do not harmonize.

Since every thought held in the conscious mind has a tendency to draw to it every other harmonious or related thought, the feelings, thoughts and emotions which claim the attention of the conscious mind are backed by a regular army of supporting soldiers who stand ready to aid them in their work.

If you place in your mind, through the principle of suggestion, the ambition to succeed in any undertaking, you will see that your latent ability is aroused and your powers automatically increased. Positive thoughts attract other positive thoughts and give you the confidence to overcome failure and achieve success. If you neutralize your negative thoughts, replace them with their positive equivalent and reinforce them through the power of suggestion, you can reach any goal you set for yourself.

Napoleon Hill's Golden Rule Magazine. February, 1919.

CHAPTER 32

When you can sincerely love everything and everybody you will be astonished at the results, for love is the magnet that attracts the best of everything. Love and praise your body, think what a wonderful machine it is and how agreeably it responds to every demand.

— Venice Bloodworth

I t never hurts to be reminded about the Golden Rule. Early in Napoleon Hill's career he was the founder and editor of his magazine aptly named *Napoleon Hill's Golden Rule*. Dr. Hill taught that being respectful and kind to others would have reciprocal benefits. What goes around comes around is a phrase often spoken flippantly, however, the message is true nonetheless. Our actions pre-determine another's actions and are a consequence of how we treat them. A smile begets a smile, road rage creates more road rage, and a pervasive atmosphere of gloom and doom can spread like a virus throughout an organization unless someone decides to "vaccinate" against it with a strong shot of PMA (positive mental attitude).

When we bring our consciousness into the forefront of our behavior and actually think about what we are doing rather than merely react, it can change our entire outcome. If we think before we respond, we can customize our response to create a new end result. If we first visualize in our mind's eye the picture perfect end result that we want to achieve, we can then create opportunities for engendering a positive reaction with those we come into contact with us on a regular basis.

"Do unto others as you would have others do unto you" is a commandment found in multiple belief systems. Since we are all part of the human family it only makes good sense to understand that people blossom when treated respectfully and die on the vine when treated with disrespect. Being human places everyone on an equal footing with everyone else. No one is more or less deserving of fair and equal treatment.

Give it a try right now. Thank the waitress sincerely for delivering your lunch, allow the driver in a hurry to pass you easily without resistance, accept the cleanup assignment for the hospitality you extended to guests with grace rather than with complaint, and go the extra mile to indicate that you are always willing to do more than you are paid to do because it is part of your work ethic to give more than expected. Sooner or later you will be recognized for your strong contribution and people will realize that you are worthy of good treatment yourself.

The Golden Rule as a Business Weapon

Dr. Napoleon Hill

It seems ridiculous to refer to the Golden Rule as a "weapon," but that is just what it is—a weapon which no resistance on earth can withstand

The Golden Rule is a powerful weapon in business, because there is so little competition in its application.

At the time of this writing, the whole world seems to have gone into the business of "profiteering," which means the same as "getting without giving fair value in return." This spirit of greed cannot long prevail. What an opportunity, then, for the farsighted men and women who will adopt the Golden Rule as their business motto now. The contract would be so noticeable that it would excite widespread comment and bring all the business that could be handled, and long after the profiteers have gone out of business, those who have applied the Golden Rule would find that they had "built their houses upon a rock."

What a glorious opportunity the labor unions have to ride to victory—permanent, profitable, bloodless victory—by applying the Golden Rule and making it their motto. Will union labor be big enough to see this opportunity and utilize it? What an opportunity the present situation offers some individual in the rank and file of labor to rise to leadership, not only of organized labor, but to the highest and most responsible leadership position the American people have to offer, by influencing labor to conduct its affairs under the Golden Rule philosophy.

There is not a situation on earth which does not offer a splendid opportunity for someone to benefit by making use of the Golden Rule.

The time is not far distant when it will be business suicide to try to conduct business under any other standard except the Golden Rule. This fact is so obvious that it seems to this writer expedient for the wise ones to fall in line now and thereby get credit for something which they will later have to do anyway.

Adopt the Golden Rule as your business motto and write it on your business stationery and in every advertisement you publish. It will pay you handsomely.

Napoleon Hill's Golden Rule Magazine. February, 1920.

Chapter 33

How would you like for one week to take one pioneer for your example and strive with his spirit inside you, to make progress on your particular problem? Maybe your week's example would carry you far. That germ might get into your system and never let up until your reach your goal.

—William H. Danforth

Many people do not qualify as leaders, but are always on the lookout for a good one. People complain of lack of leadership and yet perish the thought of stepping up to the plate themselves. Just imagine if leaders could show up on call. Wouldn't that be a wonderful circumstance to experience? But the reality of the situation is that leaders come from within the ranks of those they serve more often than not. True leaders serve because they are called to service. If a person looks at what they can get before what they can give, their leadership position will not endure.

The functions of positional leadership are designed to meet the needs of those who support a leader in their role. Imagine a pyramid as a base and consider the foundation of the structure as it rises to a pinnacle or point. The point is the culmination of the edifice, but the support is in the structure below. As with leadership, a person doesn't rise to the top without personal effort, nor does a person stay in this position without positive action. Leaders need to cultivate an alliance with the group they represent.

Consider that a good leader serves as a spokesperson for the group. This is one aspect of their role. Another equally important aspect is that they serve as a visionary and set the pace for the group to follow. The Biblical quotation, "Without vision the people perish," is a good reminder for leaders in any field to stay ahead of the norm. A leader should maintain the status quo, but also have an eye on growth and development. Leaders who are stagnant do not maintain equilibrium in the organization, but begin a downward spiral. Leaders who are in motion utilize the energy of the flow to empower themselves and their organization to new heights.

As in life, when you're green you grow, when you're ripe you rot. There can be no status quo leadership. By definition, a leader must think intelligently and take action. Nothing less is acceptable.

The Leaders and the Led

Dr. Napoleon Hill

Men and women may be divided into two classes — the leaders and the led.

Ninety-eight percent of us belong in the latter class!

What takes a person out of the latter class and places him or her in the former as one of the leaders?

Nothing but intelligent human thought, followed by intelligent action.

No one can hold for long the leadership role unless his thought is just and intelligent. Through force, trickery and deceit, an individual may become a leader for a time, but the Law of Compensation respects no person, and it eventually demands strict accountability from all leaders.

No one can long be a leader of any people without the consent and goodwill of those who are led. Bear this in mind if you would attain and permanently hold leadership in any undertaking.

This writer does not know for sure, but he strongly suspects that the wise and able leader in any undertaking will keep harmony in the ranks of those whom he is leading. May it not also be a good plan to teach those who are being led to be just and fair among themselves?

The leader who plants hatred in the hearts of his followers very closely resembles the foolish gentleman who found a frozen rattlesnake, brought it into his house, thawed it out and then was killed by its bite.

Whotsoever a man soweth, that shall he also reap.

Nero fiddled while Rome was burning. He was a leader for a time, but he didn't believe it was worthwhile to keep harmony in his ranks or to be just with his fellowmen.

You can find examples throughout history of the extremes of leadership — those who led by force and intimidation and those who were fair and just, true leaders who led with the consent of their followers. You will find that those who oppressed their people did not last for long.

In the differences between the tactics of the leader and those of the tyrant, you will find all that evolution and the history of the world has taught the human race about leadership!

Napoleon Hill's Golden Rule Magazine. March, 1919.

CHAPTER 34

My parents brought the values of country living to city life. These are still the wisest principles for sound health: clean air and water, plenty of exercise outdoors in all seasons, fresh fruits and vegetables in season, and a balance of rest and quiet, work and play. We were instilled with a deep awareness, respect, and reverence for the Creator and all created things. This connection sustains us, invigorates us, revitalizes us, and moves us through the times when health challenges appear. For me, these are still the wisest principles for sound health.

— Patsi Gately

The French psychologist, Emil Coué, gave the world a very simple formula for maintaining a sound health consciousness. He recommended the daily repetition of this sentence: "Every day in every respect, I am getting better and better." I like to substitute the word "way" for "respect" because it creates a little rhyming jingle that is easy to memorize and repeat for a positive auto-suggestion. Once the subconscious mind picks up the message and acts on it, the result is improved health. The opposite side of the coin is the statement, "If you think you are sick, you are." Which one do you want to adopt?

Our mind cannot hold two thoughts at once. The predominating thought is the one that literally impresses our subconscious mind and brings about the involuntary powerful actions that produce change on a cellular lever. If we remember the simple phrase, "thoughts are things," we know that we can create the person we want to become by first holding a positive thought in our consciousness. Once programmed, this thought will enter into our subconscious "hard drive" and enable the program to be carried out in our waking world. Keeping this in mind, it is good to note Napoleon Hill's recommendations for a healthy body. As always, Dr. Hill was ahead of his time in making a strong argument for sensible dietary guidelines.

As you read each one of the points below, ask yourself how many of these habits do you practice in your daily eating plan? If you could use a healthier lifestyle, why not consider implementing one or more of his suggestions? The tips are both easy to understand and cost-effective. What have you got to lose by trying?

Eating Habits

Dr. Napoleon Hill

This subject is worthy of an entire book, but inasmuch as there are many well written books on the subject we shall here confine ourselves to a few simple recommendations which are on the "must" list of all who would enjoy sound health.

The "MUSTS" of Correct Eating

1. First, there must be no over-eating! It over-works the heart, liver, kidneys and the sewer system. A simple way to observe this admonition is the habit of getting up from the table before one is thoroughly satisfied. The habit will be a little difficult to acquire, but once it has been developed it will pay off in big dividends, consisting in many benefits—among them a great saving in doctors' bills. Over eating is a form of intemperance which may be, and it often is, just as injurious as intemperance in drinking alcoholic beverages, or the taking of narcotics.

2. One must eat a balanced ration, consisting of at least a fair proportion of fruits and vegetables, because they contain the sixteen major mineral elements which nature requires in the building and maintenance of the physical body. No vegetable contains all of these elements; therefore, in order to provide the body with the building material it requires one must eat a variety of food that is produced by nature from the soil of the earth.

    Moreover, one must be sure that the vegetables he eats contain all the mineral elements that nature demands, which is something that cannot be determined by the appearance of the vegetable alone.

    Healthful food must be grown to order from soil that has been analyzed and is known to contain all the mineral elements which nature needs in the production of healthful food. Food that is lacking in the necessary mineral elements ferments in the alimentary canal, decays and sets up a condition known as toxic poisoning. Thus, deficient food not only fails to supply the body with the mineral elements it needs to carry on it maintenance work, but it actually creates a poison which may provide the beginning of a great variety of diseases. Some doctors have frankly admitted that most diseases begin in the alimentary canal, because of improper digestion.

3. There must be no gulping of food nor fast eating. Such methods prevent the proper mastication of the food, and also indicate a nervous mental attitude which becomes a part of the food and is carried into the blood stream.

4. There must be no eating between meals of tidbits, such as candy-bars and other sweets. If any eating between meals is done it should consist of ripe fruits, berries or raw vegetables. The better plan is to avoid between-meal eating altogether.

5. Liquor and other alcoholic beverages are on the taboo list at all times.

6. Where properly mineralized fresh vegetables are not available, the deficiency should be made up by compounded vitamins. These are available in most drug stores, but they should never be taken without a complete physical analysis by a competent doctor which will show how many vitamins are required and of what types. Vitamins contain the health-building factors of vegetation. They are the "élan vital" of all vegetation — the life-giving force.

    There is perhaps not one person in the United States who does not require at one time or another compounded vitamins, of one combination or another, to complete his or her dietary requirements. The wonders the vitamins perform in health building are many. Vitamin A dissolves kidney stones. Vitamin B-1 aids the deaf. Vitamin G softens cataracts. Vitamin C helps to master hay fever and relieves arthritis.

7. Last, but by no means least, the mind must be conditioned and prepared for eating. One should never eat while angry, or frightened, or worried. Conversation while eating should be of a pleasant nature and not too intense. Family disagreements and discipline should never take place during meal time. Fasting should be a definite form of worship in which all negative states of mind have been discarded. It should be an expression of gratitude to the Creator for having prepared so great an abundance of the necessities of life for every living creature; not an hour for ugly expressions and negative thinking.

How to Raise Your Own Salary. Napoleon Hill Associates, 1953, pp. 257–278.

CHAPTER 35

Reading through Dr. Hill's Mental Equipment Checklist, I am reminded how our physical fitness affects all the other areas of our lives—"without your health, you have nothing," as the saying goes. It's more difficult to have courage and face adversity if you aren't feeling strong. You won't have the endurance for hard work if your body isn't conditioned.

—Christopher Lake

D r. Hill states, "Tell me how you use your spare time and how you spend your money, and I will tell you where and what you will be ten years from now." This statement makes many of us cringe because we would rather focus on our best qualities than address the attributes we are lacking.

During seminars, I ask participants to rate themselves on a scale of 0–100 percent measuring the use they give to each of the 17 principles. Usually five to eight of the principles are rated very highly, and the person doing the rating feels secure in the fact that they do indeed use the success system to a large degree. Next, I ask them to circle the ones that they rated lowest. Again, there are several that they can identify. When I ask them whether they will improve greatly in their quest for success by focusing on what they are already good at, or would they be better served by working on those principles that fall well below the 50 percentile line, insight is gained. Most agree that polishing the apple does not do as much good as honing new skills that they are lacking.

Budgeting Time and Money can often have a negative ring to it. We like to speak of abundance rather than budget because budget implies lack. But, if we change the lens we use to look at life, this budgeting can be a good thing because it enables us to make the best use of our resources without wasting a thing. Waste is not positive. When we waste, we are lacking in gratitude for the gifts we have received. A by-product of abundance should never be waste.

Are you wasting some of your potential gifts by failing to incorporate the necessary skills that would contribute to their development? Persistence, practice, personal initiative, positive mental attitude, and a definite purpose are all aspects of the total success system. If you are failing could it be because you are failing to use all the necessary principles? Wouldn't you agree that most of the time we tell children to eat their vegetables before they can have dessert? It's no different with rewards as an adult. You must complete the process before you earn the prize.

Mental Equipment Checklist

Dr. Napoleon Hill

There follows a list of very desirable qualities which almost any normal and reasonable person can come to possess and exercise. The list is long and perfection may be only slowly attained. Therefore, before entering into a detailed consideration of the things you would like to have your mind and body capable of doing, let's at once enumerate those which are absolutely necessary.

1. Physical fitness is of tremendous importance for the simple reason that neither mind nor body can function well without it. Therefore, give attention to your habits of life, proper diet, healthful exercise and fresh air.

2. Courage must be the part of every man or woman who succeeds in any undertaking, especially that of selling in these trying times of intense competi-

tion after a devastating period of depression and discouragement.

3. Imagination is an absolute requisite of a successful salesman. He must anticipate situations and even objections on the part of his prospective customer. He must have such a lively imagination as to enable its operation to place him in sympathetic understanding with the position, needs, and objectives of his customer. He must almost literally stand in the other man's shoes. This takes real imagination.

4. Speech. The tone of voice must be pleasing. A high-pitched squeaky voice is irritating. Words half swallowed are hard to understand. Speak distinctly and enunciate clearly. A meek voice indicates a weak person. A firm, clean-cut, clear voice that moves with assurance and color, indicates an aggressive person with enthusiasm and aggressiveness.

5. Hard work is the only thing that will turn sales training and ability into money. No amount of good health, courage, or imagination is worth a dime unless it is put to work; and the amount of pay a salesman gets is usually fixed by the amount of very hard, intelligent work that he actually puts out. Many people side-step this factor of success.

How to Sell Your Way Through Life. Ralston Publishing Co., 1955, pp. 72–73.

CHAPTER 36

Do not hold yourself back any longer. Whatever it is that you're doing that is constructive, that is creative, go the extra mile. Don't just go the extra mile, go the second mile. Do it with all of the energy, with all of the power, with all of the love, with all of the commitment that is in your being. Do it, be it. Share yourself.
— Jack Boland

Every fall I am amazed at the amount of seeds that are produced by my four o'clocks, marigolds, and morning glories. I go outdoors with a container to collect these seeds for my spring plantings and always have a surplus to give away. Each flower not only produces enough to sustain its reproduction but an over abundance of seeds so that there is no doubt that it will survive into the next growing season.

At a recent workshop that Don Green and I were conducting in Charlottesville, Virginia, at the Boar's Head, I read Shel Silverstein's book, *The Giving Tree*. The story is about a boy and a tree that loves him. As the boy grows up, matures, and gets older, he begins to appreciate his true relationship with the tree. For all his life, the tree gave, and gave, and gave, not requiring anything in return but the boy's appreciation and possibly companionship. At one point, the boy wants to have money, so the boy asks the tree "Can you give me money?" The tree replies that it doesn't have any money, but does have apples, and the boy would be welcome to take those, sell them, and earn money. The boy does this and goes away for a time.

As Don listened to this story and its various interpretations about Going the Extra Mile, he raised his hand and asked why the boy didn't use his entrepreneurial spirit and extract the seeds from the apples, plant them, and grow an orchard that would continue to produce apples year after year? I pondered his question, and had to agree that the ongoing income from an apple orchard would certainly be more than what could be earned from the sale of a seasonal bushel of apples. Don had a good point. Sometimes the obvious can be overlooked, and with just a little entrepreneurial thinking we could become more self-sufficient! Hmmm. Instead of giving those flower seeds away, I could sell them!

Jack Boland recounts a time when he opened a book of Ralph Waldo Emerson's essays and honed in on this passage: "If you serve an ungrateful master, serve him the more, put God in your debt, every stroke shall be repaid." So, regardless of our motive, we should not hold back because the Universe takes into account our going the extra mile and sooner or later compound interest upon compound interest will be paid in full. What a promise of a reward! If for this and no other reason, we should make a firm commitment to go the extra mile, day in and day out. And, we need to be aware too of the hidden opportunities that lurk just beyond what we might see as the solution to our problems. There are orchards in apples, and the seed of an equivalent or greater benefit in every problem we decide to crack open and examine. No reason to hold back.

Advantages in Going the Extra Mile

Dr. Napoleon Hill

Some advantages for doing more than one is paid for:

1. The habit of Going the Extra Mile gives one the benefit of the law of Increasing Returns, in a variety of ways too numerous to be described here.
2. This habit places one in a position to benefit by the law of Compensation, through which no act or deed will or can be expressed without an equivalent response (after its own nature).

3. It gives one the benefit of growth through resistance and use, thereby leading to mental development and increased skill in the use of the body. (It is a well-known fact that both body and mind attain efficiency and skill through systematic discipline and use which call for the rendering of service that temporarily is not paid for.)

4. The habit develops the important factor of initiative, without which no individual ever rises above mediocrity in any calling.

5. It develops self-reliance, which is likewise an essential in all forms of personal achievement.

6. It enables an individual to profit by the law of contrast, since obviously a majority of the people do not follow the habit of doing more than they are paid for. On the contrary, they endeavor to "get by" with a minimum amount of service.

7. It helps one to master the habit of drifting aimlessly, thereby checking the habit which stands at the head of the major causes of failure.

8. It definitely aids in development of the habit of Definiteness of Purpose, which is the first principle of individual achievement.

9. It tends strongly to aid in the development of Attractiveness of Personality, thereby leading to the means by which one may relate himself to others so as to gain their friendly cooperation.

10. It often gives an individual a preferred position of relationship with others through which he may become indispensable, thereby fixing his own price on his services.

11. It ensures continuous employment, thereby serving as insurance against want in connection with the necessities of life.

12. It is the greatest of all the known methods by which the man who works for wages may promote himself to higher positions and better wages, and serves as

a practical means by which a man may attain the position of ownership of a business or industry.

13. It develops alertness of the imagination, the faculty through which one may create practical plans for the attainment of one's aims and purposes in any calling.

14. It develops a positive "mental attitude," which is one of the more important qualities that are essential in all human relationships.

15. It serves to build the confidence of others in one's integrity and general ability, which is an indispensable essential for noteworthy achievement in every calling.

16. Finally, it is a habit which one may adopt and follow on his own initiative, without being under the necessity of asking the permission of anyone to do so.

Compare these 16 definite advantages that are available to man, in return for doing more than he is paid for, with the one sole benefit (that of acquiring food necessary for existence) that is available to the other creatures of the earth through the same habit, and you will be forced to the conclusion that overwhelmingly the greater number of benefits enjoyed by man serve as adequate compensation for his development and use of this habit. This comparison substantiates your statement that it is an impossibility for one to do more than one is paid for, and for the very obvious reason that in the mere act of doing that which is constructive one acquires power that can be converted into whatever one desires.

How to Raise Your Own Salary. Napoleon Hill Associates, 1953, pp. 120–122.

Chapter 37

Perhaps the most significant decision you'll ever make is deciding your major purpose in life, what you're all about. If you have never done this, you're normal—most people don't, as we're not really educated properly to do so. But it's a must if you want to have a clear direction for your future.

—Jim Rohrbach

Nailing down the characteristics of real life leaders can be like trying to capture quicksilver once it has escaped from its container. What makes one leader charismatic and another a tyrant; one worthy of followers and another someone to be feared? Leaders are not generic, nor do they come in the "one size fits all" category. Still, for those aspiring to lead others, a person must first get their own values and beliefs in line with the mission they want to accomplish. I like to recite the Marine quote, "Leader of one, leader of many. If you can't lead one, you can't lead any." This always reminds me to begin at the beginning!

If you are looking to become a leader, first you must hitch your wagon to the proverbial star. You must focus with laser beam accuracy on what it is you want to accomplish, and this in turn will be the inspiration for those who want to go in the direction that you are moving. Once you declare your vision, either people will line up to endorse what you represent, or they will head in the other direction. So be certain as to the direction you are moving.

Next, hold the vision both at arm's length and in the distance too. Look toward the short term goals that can be accomplished quickly, and also to the long term plans in the future. Both are required. People want to participate in immediate progress, but they do not want to abandon the visionary dreams. If you can both feed the hungry today, and eradicate world hunger ten years from now, you are working on the type of plan I am talking about.

Finally, do not compromise on the big picture. The thought is the thing, as Napoleon Hill reminds us. And, there are many ways to manifest the thought physically in the here and now. Always know the direction you are moving in, but don't fret about how you travel. The mechanism is not nearly as important as the thought.

The qualities of good leadership are attainable by each of us. Consider the characteristics outlined by Napoleon Hill below. Focus on one per day. Study a biography of a person you consider to be a phenomenal leader. Discern what traits this leader possessed. Once you have the roadmap, the trip only requires that you follow the itinerary. Step into your future. Lead the way.

Qualities of a Successful Leader

Dr. Napoleon Hill

Personal initiative heads the list of qualities a successful leader must possess. These qualities are:

- Personal initiative.
- The adoption of a definite major purpose.
- A motive to inspire continuous action in pursuit of a definite major purpose.
- A master mind alliance through which you may acquire the power to attain your definite purpose.
- Self-reliance in proportion to the scope and object of your major purpose.
- Self-discipline sufficient to insure mastery of the head and the heart, and to sustain your motives until they have been realized.
- Persistence, based on the will to win.

- A well-developed imagination, controlled and directed.
- The habit of reaching definite and prompt decisions.
- The habit of basing opinions on known facts instead of relying on guesswork.
- The habit of going the extra mile.
- The capacity to generate enthusiasm at will, and to control it.
- A well-developed sense of details.
- The capacity to take criticism without resentment.
- Familiarity with the ten basic motives that inspire all human action.
- The capacity to concentrate your full attention upon one task at a time.
- Willingness to accept full responsibility for the mistakes of subordinates.
- The habit of recognizing the merits and abilities of others.
- A positive mental attitude at all times.
- The habit of assuming full responsibility for any job or task undertaken.
- The capacity for applied faith.
- Patience with subordinates and associates.
- The habit of following through with any task once begun.
- The habit of emphasizing thoroughness instead of speed.
- Dependability, the only requirement of leadership that can be stated with one word—but no less important to success on that account.

There are qualities of minor importance which leadership in many fields of endeavor may require, but those listed above are on the must list of all able leaders. Measure any successful leader by the list and observe how many of the traits he applies, although he may do so unconsciously.

PMA Science of Success. Pp. 201–203.

CHAPTER 38

If you are serious about changing your career and your life, then
get in the practice of working on your mental attitude first.
— Mike Brooks

A dmit it. At times it is difficult to maintain a positive mental attitude. Life takes its twists and turns, and sooner or later things that we label "bad" come our way. The cycle of life has both high points and low points as well. We can see this cycle played out in nature in the seasons, in the stock market, in the life span of all living things, and in the blessings and adversities that life hands to us. Without the "bad" we would not appreciate the "good." For us to know the blessings that we have received from the Creator, it is a requirement to know what lack of these gifts would be like too. Dr. Hill states, "In every adversity and defeat, there is a seed of an equal or equivalent benefit." When we ponder this thought and look for the seed of benefit, it should be no surprise that Infinite Intelligence could be handing us a real pearl of great worth. But, first we must pry open the shell to find the pearl hidden inside.

In maintaining a positive attitude it is a prerequisite that we cultivate an attitude of gratitude. Be thankful for the small gifts, and then you will be more receptive to the big ones when they show up. At night, express gratitude to the Universe for the good things that have come your way during the day. For example, you might express your gratitude at having a friendly waitress who attended you at dinner, for the gift of health insurance when you receive your flu shot, for the electric lights that permit you to read at night, for the gift of a friend who phoned or emailed you when you needed someone to talk to. You get the idea. Make a list of ten simple gifts that you received during the day, and practice positive self-talk as you drift off to sleep. I guarantee that you will be more positive in the morning when you remind yourself at night just how lucky and gifted you really are.

So, to be positive day in and day out over the long haul takes practice and endurance. It is not pre-programmed or hereditary, but the result of self-discipline. The bad news is that you have to install the hardware and software yourself, but the good news is that it will endure for a lifetime if you remember to apply it.

A Lesson from Nature

Dr. Napoleon Hill

Everything, animate or inanimate, starts out as a nucleus — a whirling bit of energy which, although so small as to defy the lens of the microscope, has the power to attract to itself whatever of a like nature it requires for its sustenance and growth.

Remember the acorn and the handful of earth. Locked up within that acorn is the germ of life, the nucleus which is capable of drawing from its surrounding elements of soil, air, water, and sunlight, the materials to build an oak tree.

Take a seed of corn or wheat; plant it in the ground and it will create a center of activity which attracts from its environment the precise balance of chemical constituents which will produce a cornstalk, or a stalk of wheat, and bring forth a reproduction of itself, according to the law of growth and increased returns.

These analogies help us to get a true picture of the power of the mind through self-suggestion. You can see how it is possible to sow a seed of desire with the subconscious mind through conscious expressed repetition of this desire... to feed and nourish this seed by the stimulus of high emotion... to germinate it by the sunshine of faith, and thus to attract to yourself from the bounteous supply of life energy in Infinite Intelligence the practical plans whereby that original seed of desire may be developed into its physical counterpart.

The law of attraction is based upon the principle of growth from the vitality which is inherent in the seed (idea or desire) itself. Every seed has, in itself, a potentially perfect plant. Every worthy desire has in it the potential power for its perfect fulfillment. If a seed is to germinate and produce a crop after its own kind, it must be planted in fertile soil, it must have nourishment, and it must have sunshine to ripen it for harvest.

Your subconscious mind can be compared to a fertile garden spot wherein may be planted the seed of your definite purpose, by means of a burning desire which imparts the initial energy into the nucleus of your definite purpose, and causes it to enlarge and grow. Now we have explained how the seed may be nourished and cultivated by persistent action according to your plans and through repeated instructions to your subconscious. Also how you may attract the vitalizing influence of Infinite Intelligence and focus it on the object of your desire. Here you have the whole process laid before you. It is a process which is going on all around you in countless forms of life. It is not a matter of theory. It is a demonstrated fact. You have only to adapt it to your own definite purpose.

PMA Science of Success. Pp. 106–107.

CHAPTER 39

Don't ignore hate. It can tell you all sorts of things about your weaknesses and vulnerabilities and the environment in which you find yourself. But once your hate has informed you of the danger or vulnerability, stop hating and start taking positive actions to overcome your vulnerability or remove yourself from the situation or person inspiring your hate.

—Elie Alperstein

Being human, none of us is perfect. Trials and tribulations enter our lives on a regular basis, and many of us fall out of favor with our higher selves daily as we commit sins of omission or fail to act in our most positive manner. Still, we can pick ourselves up and dust ourselves off as we begin anew each time we decide that with a positive mental attitude we can yet become the best person we are capable of being.

When Dr. Hill teaches the positive and negative emotions that propel us toward action, he notes that these are like self-igniters or sparkplugs that get us to move. As long as we are aware that negativity in any shape or form is not the desired outcome, we are able to redirect the energy and use it for good. It is the transmutation of the negative energy—the alchemy of changing negative emotions into positive actions—that is the miracle in the making. This miracle is something everyone can cause to happen because by thinking and conceptualizing a positive outcome, we can bring it forward into our lives. Turning a negative into a positive is a result of shifting our thought and belief system from bad to good. It requires thinking and awareness, but when you realize that you control the outcome—even in a bad situation that you may have created yourself—you have the power to produce a positive from a negative.

Feel the power? It is really there. Just decide once and for all that even if there have been some "mistakes" or steps in the wrong direction, these experiences can be viewed as tools for learning and can be used to redirect us toward the positive path our lives are meant to take. The duality of the Universe is evident in creation. Without the dark side there would be no light. Use the tools you have been given to perfect yourself.

The Devil's Workshop

Dr. Napoleon Hill

In addition to the Six Basic Fears, there is another evil by which people suffer. It constitutes a rich soil in which the seeds of failure grow abundantly. It is so subtle that its presence often is not detected. This affliction cannot properly be classed as a fear. It is more deeply seated and more often fatal than all of the six fears. For want of a better name, let us call this evil susceptibility to negative influences.

Men who accumulate great riches always protect themselves against this evil! The poverty-stricken never do! Those who succeed in any calling must prepare their minds to resist the evil. If you are reading this philosophy for the purpose of accumulating riches, you should examine yourself very carefully, to determine whether you are susceptible to negative influences. If you neglect this self-analysis, you will forfeit your right to attain the object of your desires.

...

You can easily protect yourself against highway robbers, because the law provides organized cooperation for your benefit, but this "seventh basic evil" is more difficult to master, because it strikes when you are not aware of its presence, when you are asleep, and while you are awake.

138

Moreover, its weapon is intangible, because it consists of merely—a state of mind. This evil is also dangerous because it strikes in as many different forms as there are human experiences. Sometimes it enters the mind through the well meant words of one's own relatives. At other times, it bores from within, through one's own mental attitude. Always it is as deadly as poison, even though it may not kill as quickly.

To protect yourself against negative influences, whether of your own making, or the result of the activities of negative people around you, recognize that you have a will-power, and put it into constant use, until it builds a wall of immunity against negative influences in your own mind.

Think and Grow Rich. Ballantine Books, 1996, pp. 243-244.

CHAPTER 40

Back in 2002, I attended a seminar at the Napoleon Hill World Learning Center in Hammond, Indiana, and my life changed. In that learning environment, upon re-evaluating myself for the zillionth time in terms of my knowledge and practice of Dr. Hill's philosophy, I discovered a key component of my Definite Major Purpose in Life, which had gone largely unnoticed up until that time, although I had been developing it sporadically all along.

—John Stutte

The last thing a person wants to hear after a major setback is that it is only temporary and he can always pull himself up by his bootstraps! Have you ever tried doing that? It almost seems pointless. The sheer law of gravity prevents any upward mobility when it is done in this fashion. Standing on the floor, just try grabbing those shoelaces (closest things we have to bootstraps) and pulling upward. Ludicrous or not, the thought is still the thing—the mechanism is not nearly as important. The shoelaces will probably give way, but you get the point. You can overcome any adversity as long as you maintain a positive mental attitude and set your sights on achieving your desire. At least now you are laughing about it!

Many people have failed in their initial attempts to scale certain peaks, but they have tried and tried again until they eventually succeeded. Has the peak changed and become less of a challenge? No, the person has changed and eventually grew into the challenge. It was the next or subsequent try that the challenge was overcome. Our failures are learning tools that help us inch toward the direction of our goal *if* we heed the lesson intertwined in the failure.

Recall how you learned to walk, ride a bicycle, drive a car, dance, and on and on. It was never spontaneous—but it was a series of steps that were imperfect and erratic from the start. Did you give up? No. It just took a decision to do it, time to practice, and the repetition of the action over and over and over again until your subconscious mind took over the habit and made it an unconscious action.

Think about it. Give your thoughts some space to mature and grow. Think the big, bigger, and the very biggest thoughts that you can conjure up! Then find the action, the mechanism, that will carry you to your goals one step at a time. Who knows? You might find yourself stepping right into your wildest dreams. Ah, how sweet it is!

Climb Over Your Failures

Dr. Napoleon Hill

There are exceptions to this rule; a few people know from experience the soundness of persistence. They are the ones who have not accepted defeat as being anything more than temporary. They are the ones whose desires are so persistently applied that defeat is finally changed into victory. We who stand on the side-lines of life see the over-whelmingly large number who go down in defeat, never to rise again. We see the few who take the punishment of defeat as an urge to greater effort. These, fortunately, never learn to accept life's reverse gear. But what we do not see, what most of us never suspect of existing, is the silent but irresistible power which comes to the rescue of those who fight on in the face of discouragement. If we speak of this power at all we call it persistence, and let it go at that. One thing we all know, if one does not possess persistence, one does not achieve noteworthy success in any calling.

As these lines are being written, I look up from my work, and see before me, less than a block away, the great mysterious Broadway, the "Graveyard of Dead Hopes," and the "Front Porch of Opportunity." From all over the world people have come to Broadway, seeing fame, fortune, power, love, or whatever it is that human beings call success. Once in a great while someone steps out from the long procession of seekers, and the world hears that another person has mastered Broadway. But Broadway is not easily nor quickly conquered. She acknowledges talent, recognizes genius, pays off in money, only after one has refused to quit.

Then we know he has discovered the secret of how to conquer Broadway. The secret is always inseparably attached to one word, persistence!

Think and Grow Rich. Ballantine Books, 1996, p. 155.

CHAPTER 41

It all begins with you: *Do you believe that you are worthy and deserving of success? Many people don't, so they flounder in mediocrity. Have you ever heard yourself saying, in relation to top achievers in your field, "Y'know, I'm good ... but I'm not that good." That's an indicator that you lack faith in your ability to be among the best.*

— Jim Rohrbach

When you lose faith, where do you go to find it? If you could answer that question the world would beat a path to your doorstep. At many stages in a person's life faith seems to disappear just when it is needed the most. An illness or death in the family, a loss of job, a personal illness, sudden depression, financial setbacks, expectations that remain unfulfilled, and numerous other "losses" can cause a person to doubt what before had been a strong belief in the good things in life.

Fear and faith cannot co-exist. Either you are fearful or you are faithful. One is a negative belief and the other is positive. Faith defies logic, but it can be accelerated if it is put into practice. Applied faith is taking action in the direction of your belief. This means that you "act as if" the outcome you believe in is already a fact. Let no doubt or disbelief enter into your thinking because that negative thought will seep into your subconscious mind and allow an element of fear to launch a counter attack against what you truly want.

If you have a poverty mentality, you will not produce wealth. If you are cautious in creating friendships, you will not acquire wealth in relationships. If you withhold on your job, your job will never be fulfilling for you. If you fail to be of service, you will receive no recognition for

Applied Faith

going the extra mile. When you think thoughts of lack, that lack is what you attract into your life.

When creating a representation for me of applied faith, artist Michael Telapary produced the image above.

In discussing this image, Michael pointed out to me that the person walking the tightrope has no balance beam—rather, her higher self serves in this capacity. As we view the image, it can be seen that her "higher self" offers the support that she needs to cross the ravine. And, she would never have attempted the crossing if she was not certain that she would reach the other side.

Likewise, in our lives we must rely on only ourselves to muster up the faith that we need to get though life. The setbacks in life are no excuse to abandon our belief system. We need to envision the best possible outcome given the circumstances, and then walk into our future one faithful step at a time. The alternative is not acceptable for anyone who espouses a positive mental attitude.

No One is "Doomed" to Bad Luck

Dr. Napoleon Hill

From this statement, you will understand that the subconscious mind will translate into its physical equivalent a thought impulse of a negative or destructive nature, just as readily as it will act upon thought impulses of a positive or constructive nature. This accounts for the strange phenomenon which so many millions of people experience, referred to as "misfortune," or "bad luck."

There are millions of people who believe themselves "doomed" to poverty and failure, because of some strange force over which they believe they have no control. They are the creators of their own "misfortunes," because of this negative belief, which is picked up by the subconscious mind, and translated into its physical equivalent.

This is an appropriate place at which to suggest again that you may benefit, by passing on to your subconscious mind, any desire which you wish translated into its physical equivalent, or monetary equivalent, in a state of expectancy or belief that the transmutation will actually take place. Your belief, or faith, is the element which determines the action of your subconscious mind. There is nothing to hinder you from "deceiving" your subconscious mind when giving it instructions through autosuggestion, as I deceived my son's subconscious mind.

To make this "deceit" more realistic, conduct yourself just as you would if you were already in possession of the material thing which you are demanding, when you call upon your subconscious mind.

The subconscious mind will transmute into its physical equivalent, by the most direct and practical media available, any order which is given to it in a state of belief, or faith that the order will be carried out.

Surely, enough has been stated to give a starting point from which one may, through experiment and practice, acquire the ability to mix faith with any order given to the subconscious mind. Perfection will come through practice. It cannot come by merely reading instructions.

It is essential for you to encourage the positive emotions as dominating forces of your mind, and discourage— and eliminate— negative emotions.

A mind dominated by positive emotion, becomes a favorable abode for the state of mind known as faith. A mind so dominated may, at will, give the subconscious mind instructions, which it will accept and act upon immediately.

Think and Grow Rich. Ballantine Books, 1996, pp. 51–52.

CHAPTER 42

Giving advice where it is not needed or wanted is probably the most prevalent form of Selfish Giving. It often undermines the self-esteem of the individual receiving this "gift" and will generally poison the atmosphere between the "giver" and recipient.

— Elie Alperstein

The underlying message in Dr. Hill's PMA (Positive Mental Attitude) Science of Success Course is that giving begets getting. Only when a natural flow is created does the process speed up and good results happen. Opening up to creativity by allowing personal interests and talents to develop without barriers or criticism benefits everyone. Little do we know where the real solution lies. Our way may not always be the best way. When given a chance for personal expression without criticism, unique ideas can flow freely and possibly contribute toward improved decision making. When held back due to fear, the best ideas may never see the light of day.

It has been said that Going the Extra Mile is the master key to real success. It supports all the other basic principles because by helping others you invariably bring extra benefits to yourself. Magically, these benefits often come from completely unexpected sources. Consequently your own life will become richer in ways you may not now even begin to imagine.

Are you looking for more rewards? Then start giving to get. In *Think and Grow Rich*, Dr. Hill states that you must "determine exactly what you intend to give in return for the money you desire." He adds parenthetically that there "is no such reality as 'something for nothing.'" In addition, he indicates that the giving should start well before you acquire your personal "riches." In fact, you must give before you receive. This is a natural law and follows the pattern that was established by Infinite Intelligence. Whether we like it or not, we need to apply the exact formula prior to being the recipient of what we desire most from life.

Think about giving. Consider what gifts only you can give. Next, go about giving away your special talents in exchange for the life you have always only imagined.

Give to Receive

Dr. Napoleon Hill

Things you give to others, through expression, are the only things you are able to retain, remember, or keep for yourself. Any gems of thought or wisdom which you are anxious to remember, you must repeatedly give to others, or they will elude your grasp at the critical moment. Here is a simple way to test the truth of what has been said. Listen to a good story someone tells you, one worth remembering, one you would like to tell others. Do you know that if you do not tell it to someone right away you will forget it yourself? And do you know that if you do tell it, not only to one person, but to many persons, you will never forget it?

You have heard of the saying, It's better to give than to receive. Here is one place where this is literally and particularly true, because in order to retain the understanding of this or any other subject you are studying, you must give it away to someone else. That is, share it, explain it, pass it along to another person. If you try to hoard it to yourself, you will forget some of the subtle points which may be important at a certain place in your career. Share these principles with others, not the details of your purpose or plan. These details you are cautioned to share only with the greatest discretion and to keep strictly to yourself at certain times.

Giving is a form of expression and giving is living. Let us read a story which perfectly illustrates this point. The story has been adapted from a book by Bruce Barton.

There are two seas in Palestine. One, the Sea of Galilee, is fresh and fish live in it. Trees spread their branches over it and stretch out their thirsty roots to sip of its nourishing water. Christ loved this spot. He looked out across its silver surface when He spoke. And on a rolling plain not far away, He fed 5,000 on loaves and fish from this very sea. The river Jordan fills this sea with sparkling water from the hills and then flows on south into another sea. Here is no splash of fish, no fluttering leaf, no song of bird, no children's laughter. Travelers choose another route unless they are on urgent business. The air hangs heavy above its waters, and neither man nor beast nor fowl will drink of them.

What makes this mighty difference in these neighboring seas? Not the river Jordan. It empties the same good water into both. Not the soil on which they lie; nor the country about. No, none of these; but there is a difference. The Sea of Galilee receives, but does not keep the Jordan. For every drop that flows into it, another drop flows out. The giving and receiving are in equal measure. The other sea is selfish, hoarding its income jealously. Every drop it gets, it keeps. The Sea of Galilee gives and lives. The Dead Sea gives nothing. It is indeed dead. There are two kinds of people in this world—just as there are two seas in Palestine.

In this business of becoming successful, you will find you will need both hands. One hand will be stretched upward, to receive the blessing of Infinite Intelligence, with the other extended down and outward, sharing and giving to others who are helping you in the climb. No one ever achieved outstanding success without the cooperation of others; and you realize, of course, that you must give something in return for this cooperation.

PMA *Science of Success*. Educational Edition, pp. 23–24.

CHAPTER 43

I unashamedly describe myself as a formerly shy, low self-esteem underachiever with a bad attitude—in other words, I was a pretty normal young adult. You may be able to relate to that, along with feeling lost, confused, scared, frustrated, and depressed about your prospects for the future.

—Jim Rohrbach

Ask the man on the street, "Who is an educated person?" and you will surely receive a variety of answers. People might describe an educated person as a caring person, a scholarly person, a "schooled" person, a giving person, a considerate person, a noble person, a credible person, or even a "stuck up" person, and the list can go on and on. Take a moment now, yourself, and jot down all the characteristics of an educated person that come readily to mind. Next, you may try ranking your answers in order, highest to lowest. This is an interesting task because it does not necessarily describe an educated person; instead it details what importance you place on characteristics relating to education in your own world view. This disclosure can provide evidence as to why you are or are not where you want to be in your career or job.

Have you been affected lately by the economy? Have you lost employment? Have you been successful in your search for a new job? Are you able to transition from one job to another without long delays? Are you skilled, versatile, and adaptable to new work assignments?

If any of these questions apply to you, then it might be a good idea to consider the role education has played in shaping your working career. Education supplies you with tools to develop into skills that you personally sharpen through practice. Your versatility plus your record of on the job performance usually determines your longevity and/or employability. These factors are keyed in to education.

Education comes in many shapes and sizes. You can get it through experience, earn it in schools, qualify for it by completing a plan of study in a chosen program, but you can't inherit it! You must put in the effort yourself and then utilize what you know to carve out a place for yourself to grow.

Your education is yours for a lifetime. Why not invest in yourself more? Be a lifelong learner and profit in more ways than monetary income by your overall investment. Why not Think and Grow Rich? You have nothing to lose, and a life to gain.

Who is an Educated Person?

Dr. Napoleon Hill

Organized thought leads to spiritual and mental growth provided it is expressed through action. One does not grow spiritually or mentally by thought alone. Growth is the result of thought expressed through voluntary and definitely controlled habits of actions.

Ability, in its most effective form, is the result of thought expressed through organized action. Theory forms a helpful background for ability, but it is not enough to insure success. That is why the college graduate must acquire practical experience before he becomes a man of ability. Theoretical learning is an essential foundation of education, but it is only a foundation. An educated person is one who has developed his mind through a combination of theory and practice so that he can shape any set of circumstances to meet the requirements of his desires and deeds.

There is no school which equals the good old "University of Experience." This is one school where "cribbing" is not possible. One either graduates on merit, or does not graduate at all, and the teacher is the student himself. Skill is developed in every calling through the coordination of the faculties of the mind and the physical body. Such coordination is attained through controlled habits. But unless a man becomes action conscious, he will never become an organized thinker. He may think from morning until night, but he will never build a bridge, or manage an industry successfully, unless he acquires the habit of putting his theories to the test through action. Right here is where many men deceive themselves by believing that are organized thinkers. I have heard many men say, "I have been thinking of doing this or that, but so far, I have found no way to do it." The main weakness of such men is that they have left out of their thinking one important factor—physical action expressed through definiteness of purpose.

If a man wishes to do something he should begin right where he is. Many will say, "What shall I use for tools? Where will I get the necessary working capital? Who will help me?" Men who accomplish anything worthy of mention usually begin before everything they need is at hand. I have never yet been entirely ready for anything that I have undertaken, and I doubt if anyone else ever has been.

PMA Science of Success. Educational Edition, pp. 322–323.

CHAPTER 44

Symbolic systems can be anything from an actual symbol, a religious belief system, language of any kind, a simple repeatable story, and even Napoleon Hill's seventeen success principles. Symbolic systems have helped individuals and even nations survive great adversity including harsh imprisonment and prolonged exile.

— Uriel "Chino" Martinez

Have you ever heard someone speak and during the talk have an idea, phrase or sentence leap out in front of you and capture your full attention? Well, this past Sunday it happened to me. I was listening to a sermon about people who have made a contribution to our world. Each time the pastor began a new story, he asked for a show of hands as to whether or not the congregation had ever heard of the person whose life's mission he was relating. Each time no hands went up. Then, he continued by asking if we had heard certain sensational stories reported by the media, and everybody had. In conclusion, he brought his real message home by stating, "Never let other people tell your story." His point was that we have to be on guard and collectively proud enough to make certain that an accurate story is being reported when we know the subject matter. Hmmm. Have you ever dropped the ball on this one? I have.

Oftentimes we exchange truth for convenience, for deciding not to rock the boat. I am all for choosing the battles that I care to fight, but it doesn't hurt to be reminded that inaccurate representations of the truth begin with one lie at a time until there is a groundswell of wrong information being substituted for the truth. Each of us needs to be accountable for the stories people create about us and the real contributions that we make. Timidity, fear, superstition, loss of courage, and a thousand other reasons can keep us from making a statement, but peace of mind only comes by knowing that individually we have contributed our important part to the collective truth.

What good have you done? Don't be afraid to take credit by telling others first before someone negates, modifies or "borrows" your contribution. It has been said that each of us will be only accountable for the one life we are given. As for me, I hope that when I stand in judgment I can respond positively about the contributions that I have made and that I have had the courage of my convictions not to bury them under a rug. Each one of us can't do what all of us are capable of doing collectively. So, in order to remain on the path of our own choosing, make certain that when confronted with information you use the only question Napoleon Hill advises us to use: "How do you know?" Demand to see the evidence, and if it is not available, draw your own conclusion. Consider Napoleon Hill's detailed advice too when drawing conclusions about the accuracy of anything you hear or read:

1. Is the writer a recognized authority on the subject covered?
2. Did the writer have a motive other than that of imparting accurate information when he wrote the book?
3. Is the writer a professional whose business is that of influencing public opinion?
4. Has the writer a profit interest in the subjects on which he writes?
5. Is the writer a person with sound judgment, and not a fanatic on the subject on which he writes?
6. Are there readily accessible sources from which the writer's statements may be checked and verified?
7. Do the writer's statements harmonize with common sense and experience?

In following the above guidelines, you will strengthen your resolve to get to the truth and in turn develop the necessary courage to tell you own story! Don't be a bystander in your life's story. Take the lead role. You earned it.

Peace of Mind Can Be Attained Only by a Positive Mental Attitude

Dr. Napoleon Hill

Peace of mind is one of the most sought after blessings in life. As is true of everything of value, you must pay a price to obtain it. And the price required is the continual and consistent maintenance of a positive mental attitude. If you will pay this price, you will receive the following blessings, all of which result in peace of mind:

· Freedom from want.
· Freedom from superstition.
· Freedom from fear in all of its forms.
· Freedom from the common weakness of seeking something for nothing.
· The habit of doing your own thinking.
· The habit of frequent self-inspection from within, to determine what changes of character are necessary.
· The habit of developing sufficient courage and inherent honesty with yourself to look at life as a realist.
· The habit of discouraging both greed and the desire for power at the expense of others.
· The habit of helping others to help themselves.
· Recognition of the truth that the universal power of Infinite Intelligence is available to all who will learn how to use it.
· Freedom from anxiety over what may happen to you after death.
· Freedom from all desire for revenge.
· The habit of going the extra mile in all human relationships.

- Knowledge of yourself—the you which cannot be seen in a mirror; an understanding of who you are and what your virtues and abilities are.
- Freedom from discouragement.
- The habit of thinking in terms of your highest and noblest objectives.
- The habit of looking for the seed of equivalent benefit in every adversity.
- The habit of taking life in your stride, neither shrinking from the disagreeable nor over-indulging in the pleasant.
- The habit of starting where you stand to accomplish your goals.
- The habit of conquering petty misfortunes rather than being mastered by them.
- The joy of doing, rather than merely possessing.
- The habit of making life pay off on your terms, in values of your choosing.
- The habit of giving before trying to get.
- The privilege of engaging in a labor of love of your own choice.

These are some of the joys which one receives from peace of mind by exercising a positive mental attitude. A review of this list will also convince you that men with positive mental attitudes are never found in a rut. And it will also be evident to you that another blessing which can be achieved by maintaining a positive mental attitude is the attainment of success in your chosen field of endeavor.

PMA *Science of Success.* Pp. 235-236.

CHAPTER 45

When the thrill of the season turns to stress and you're in need of some calm, quiet, and introspection, we hope you'll come to the Foundation's new website, NapHill.org.

— Christopher Lake

Having an attitude of gratitude should be as habit-forming as brushing one's teeth. If we have to stop and think about how to express gratitude we have not assimilated it into our higher selves. Dr. Hill tells us that if we acknowledge the Law of Cosmic Habitforce and its unchanging pattern we can put it to work on a subconscious level. By making positive choices we create a template or pattern for the development of permanent habits—like grooves on old LP records. Through repetition we carve these grooves into our psyche and soon enough Cosmic Habitforce takes over and we literally perform to our programmed ability on autopilot. The saying "practice makes perfect" has real application when repetition is the key. Just be certain that you are practicing and recording good habits so that bad ones do not take possession of your subconscious programming.

Gratitude is one habit worth developing. It assists us in cultivating and maintaining a positive mental attitude. When we make a conscious mental shift to see the good in the world, the negative aspects do not seem as glaring or as demanding of our attention. Truth is, what we think about, we become. And, as we think on the positive things, our life—no matter where we begin or currently find ourselves—moves toward a positive focus. There is good in everything—even if it is only a seed that points us in a positive direction.

This holiday season, focus on finding things to praise rather than things to complain or worry about. Each of us has numerous concerns in our lives that could cause depression if we allowed the negative thoughts to fester. Why go there? Instead, decide to look to the small, hidden light within that if nurtured could become a flame of inspiration. Don't snuff it out. Light candle after candle mentally until you are able to eradicate the darkness within. It is a choice. See the good or see the bad. You decide.

Let's have a call to action this season of giving. Rather than having unfulfilled good intentions, make it a daily habit to do some little gesture or action that will bring joy to another person. It doesn't have to cost money either. Speaking powerfully positive words of praise to someone in need of a boost is a priceless gift and cannot be purchased at any cost. Making a phone call just to see how someone is doing, spending time with a loved one, or being on cleanup patrol after the holiday feast, are just some things that can be done without spending a dime. Do something daily, and after a month of this type of activity you will have created a positive groove in your mental recording that will continue to play the attitude of gratitude message.

This benefits you the most because next your attitude will become and remain more and more positive. It is truly the gift that you give to yourself and it keeps on giving because of the Law of Cosmic Habit-force. Be good to yourself—give first, and then receive the blessings of your repeated actions. The rewards are worth it.

Give Thanks Every Day

Dr. Napoleon Hill

Many successful men and women claim they are "self-made." But the fact is that no one reaches the pinnacle without help. Once you have set your definite major goal for success—and taken your first steps to achieve it—you find yourself receiving help from many unexpected quarters. You must be prepared to give thanks for both the human and Divine help you receive.

Gratitude is a beautiful word. It is beautiful because it describes a state of mind that is deeply spiritual in nature. It enhances one's personality with magnetic charm, and it is the master key that opens the door to the magic powers and the beauty of Infinite Intelligence. Gratitude, like other traits of the pleasing personality, is simply a matter of habit. But it's also a state of mind. Unless you sincerely feel the gratitude you express, your words will be hollow and empty — and sound as phony as the sentiment you offer.

Gratitude and graciousness are closely akin. By consciously developing a sense of gratitude, your personality will become more courtly, dignified and gracious. Never let a day pass without a few minutes spent in giving thanks for your blessings. Remember that gratitude is a matter of comparison. Compare circumstances and events against what they might have been. You'll become aware that no matter how bad things are, they could be much worse — and you'll be grateful they aren't.

Three phrases should be among the most common in your daily usage. They are "Thank you," "I'm grateful..." and "I appreciate..."

Be thoughtful. Try to find new and unique ways to express your gratitude. Not necessarily in material gifts, however. Time and effort are more precious, and the amount of these you dispense in showing gratefulness will be well worthwhile.

And don't forget to be thankful to those who are closest to you — your wife or husband, other relatives, and those you associate with daily, whom you might tend to neglect. You are probably more indebted to them than you realize.

Gratitude takes on new meaning — new life and power — when spoken aloud. Your family probably knows you are grateful for their faith and hope in you. But tell them so! Frequently! You'll find a new spirit pervading the household.

Make your gratitude creative. Make it work for you. For example, have you ever thought of writing the boss a simple note telling him how much you like your job and how grateful you are for the opportunities it offers? The shock power of such creative gratitude will bring you to his attention — and could even bring you a raise. Gratitude is infectious. He might catch the bug and find concrete ways of expressing his gratefulness for the good services you are rendering.

Remember there's always something to be grateful for. Even the prospect who turns down a salesman should be thanked for the time he spent listening. He'll be more likely to buy next time.

Gratitude costs nothing. But it's a big investment in the future.

Success Unlimited. November, 1961, pp. 27–28.

CHAPTER 46

We often find ourselves in situations not of our making. We are born into families, communities, and cultures not of our choosing. But despite wherever we may find ourselves, Dr. Hill provides us with an optimistic philosophy in which Man has the ability to create for himself a better life by using the one gift which separates him from everything else in creation: his Creative Mind.

— Eliezer Alperstein

None of us can do everything, but each of us can do little things with great pride and enthusiasm. Situations can cause a person to become overwhelmed at the enormity of the tasks at hand. When this occurs, many people figuratively freeze in their tracks and are incapable of doing a thing to resolve or improve their situation. A case in point could be dealing with an overdue bill, cleaning out the refrigerator, or beginning an assignment that you dread. Each of these tasks is different, yet equal because they have a common denominator—inaction. Failure to act often causes a situation to worsen rather than work toward resolution of the "problem."

How many times has someone told you that it can't be done? Listen to their litany of reasons as to why something couldn't or shouldn't happen. Just hearing the recitation drags down your "can do" spirit into the pits of despair. Well, Hill's philosophy is a "pull yourself up by your own bootstraps" philosophy, and unless you commit to finding a way it can be done with *you* doing it, you will never experience the positive outcomes in life that Dr. Hill foresaw for you and everyone else. Throughout Dr. Hill's material we are immersed in an attitude of positve action, not reaction or inaction. The difference in our outcome in life comes in the doing, not in thinking about doing, or questioning

160

what to do. Although each step is important, it is the "grabbing the tiger by the tail doing" that makes things progress in life.

What tigers are you chasing? Today, right now, decide to stop that tiger in his tracks and get him tamed down. Once you get that tiger to stand still for your evaluation, you can determine what terrain will best suit your needs and his needs to not only survive but thrive in life. Then, you can get him placed in the best housing possible — the mansion that you create in your mind for every good thing now and to come. There is ample room, so don't delay. Act on those problems, and watch your confidence grow to the size of your dreams.

A Word of Caution

Dr. Napoleon Hill

Keep your major purpose and your plans for attaining it to yourself except in connection with your master mind groups. The reason for this is twofold:

1. Telling many persons, indiscriminately, will allow negative thinking persons to throw stumbling blocks in your path, or to discourage you from attempting to achieve your definite major purpose.
2. Too much talking about your definite major purpose may tend to dissipate the intensity of your desire to achieve your goal.

Either eventually would tend to destroy your enthusiasm and possibly even deter you from further efforts to achieve your definite major purpose.

So far as we are able to tell, this law of cosmic habit-force is absolutely neutral, just like the subconscious section of the human mind through which it operates. It will accept and carry out a negative pattern as readily as it will a positive one. If you allow the fear of criticism, doubt and other people's negative suggestions to take shape in your mind, it will blot out the picture of your major purpose.

The reason for emphasizing this point is that it is a common tendency of people to boast and to express their greatest enthusiasm in the future tense, by telling what they are going to do. When you speak of your ambitions, if at all, use the past tense, after they have become accomplishments and are not just words.

A word of caution: Do not make the mistake of assuming that because you do not understand these principles completely, they are not sound. Follow the instructions and you will be adopting the method used by some of the greatest leaders ever produced. These instructions call for no effort that you cannot easily put forth. They make no demand on your abilities with which the average person cannot comply.

PMA Science of Success. P. 500.

CHAPTER 47

Central to embracing Hill's philosophy is the understanding of thinking positively, or the subconscious channeling of positive mental energy to think more affirmatively about our own human undertakings, whether it be at work, hobbies, relationships, or play. One must constantly look to what one shall be as opposed to what they are now. Without mastering a positive mental attitude toward challenging goals, they are often lost to the negative side of mental energy.

—Jack Kennedy

A quotation by Susan L. Taylor that echoes Napoleon Hill states, "The mind is a prolific author. What you believe—along with the actions you take—composes your life. At this moment our lives reflect where we have been in consciousness and what we have done with our time."

The ingredients that nature uses to create all things are time, space, energy, matter, and intelligence according to Hill. He states that the "same law which holds our earth in its orbit and relates it to all other planets in their orbits, both in time and space, relates human beings to one another in exact conformity with the nature of their own thoughts."

This brief discourse on the Universe reminds us that although we are placed in a system that operates uniformly whether we understand its operations or not, we can still use the natural laws to assist us in our journey toward success. Fundamental principles can guide us to our mission in life, and can assist us in streamlining the process if we follow the universal pattern established by the Creator. Dr. Hill worked steadfastly to uncover these principles and then to relate them in practical, layman's terminology, so that everyone interested in the secrets of success would have no farther to look.

The end of the journey for each one of us is the culmination of our earthly mission. For those of us who believe we are put here to fulfill a divine purpose, Dr. Hill's classic books *Think and Grow Rich* and *Law of Success* serve as guides for our journey. Although the map is not the territory, it is helpful to get an overview of the journey that we are on for life. The balance in a person's life comes from understanding the cycle of living. Just as with any recipe, if you read it accurately, purchase the right ingredients, and follow the step-by-step instructions, you will end up with what you have decided to create. Life is a creative art. Be a visionary and cook up a good one!

No Limits

Dr. Napoleon Hill

There are no limitations to the power of the mind save only those which the individual establishes for himself, or permits to be established by the influences outside of himself.

Truly, whatever the mind can *conceive* and *believe*, the mind can *achieve!*

Study well the three key words in the foregoing sentence because they epitomize the sum and the substance of this entire chapter.

Your success in the application of the mind-conditioning formula presented in this chapter will depend very largely upon the mental attitude in which you apply it. If you BELIEVE you will get satisfactory results, you will get them.

When you give directives to your subconscious mind, through the statement herein which was prepared for that purpose, you may hasten success by repeating the statement in the form of a prayer, and thereby place the entire power of your religious BELIEF back of your statement.

The word BELIEF is symbolic of a power that has no limitations within reason and we find evidence of its influence wherever we find people who have achieved noteworthy success in any calling.

Thomas A. Edison BELIEVED he could perfect an incandescent electric lamp, and that belief carried him successfully through the ten thousand failures before he got the answer for which he had been searching.

Marconi BELIEVED the ether could be made to carry the vibrations of sound without the use of wires, and that belief carried him through many failures until he was finally rewarded by triumph, and gave the world its first wireless means of communication.

Columbus BELIEVED he would find land in an uncharted portion of the Atlantic Ocean, and he sailed on and on until he found it, despite the threatened mutiny of his sailors who were not so blessed as he with the capacity for BELIEF.

Madame Schumann-Heink BELIEVED she could become a great opera singer, although her singing teacher had advised her to go back to her sewing machine and be content as a seamstress. Her BELIEF rewarded her with success.

Helen Keller BELIEVED she could learn to talk despite the fact that she lost her use of speech, sight, and hearing, and her BELIEF restored her speech and helped her to become a shining example of encouragement to all people who are tempted to give up in despair because of some physical affliction.

Henry Ford BELIEVED he could build a horseless buggy that would provide rapid transportation at small cost, and despite the far-flung cry of "crackpot" and the skepticism of the world, he belted the earth with the product of his BELIEF, and made himself immensely wealthy.

Madame Marie Curie BELIEVED that radium metal existed and gave herself the task of finding its source, despite the fact that no one had ever seen radium and no one knew where to start looking for it. Her BELIEF finally revealed the source of that precious metal.

You Can Work Your Own Miracles. Ballantine Books, 1971, pp. 144–146.

CHAPTER 48

Best and happiest of all, the Time before him was his own, to make amends in!

— Charles Dickens

This holiday season I had the gift of being treated to tickets to a local symphony performance. Music of the season was performed, and as expected Santa even made his appearance. As Santa and the conductor read letters from area children, the song "Greensleeves" was softly played in the background. Some letters were lighthearted, some were tearful, and some were thought-provoking. Each letter followed the same Christmas Wish format however, and answered the following questions:

1. What I would like for myself,
2. What I would like for my family, and
3. What I would like for the world.

As I listened to Santa reading the letters, I reflected on the questions myself. Those children who thought expansively with their gifts to the world seemed to have generous hopes for their families and themselves too. Little wonder that at any age if we comprehend the big picture of how the world should be, our little picture begins to take shape, and we can then impact the world. Somehow, it works best in reserve. Little to big, first things first, and then the very biggest results can follow right on schedule.

Why not take a moment and answer these Santa questions for yourself? Begin with the end in mind and answer question number three first. Most people would respond that we would like world peace. If this is true for you, you might next consider ways that you can create more peace and harmony here and now in your family. This is not to be a "wish" list but a "do" list. What are you going to do today to create more peace and harmony in your family? And, lastly, what are you going to gift yourself? Make sure that you have your world in order first before you accept the job of ordering someone else's universe. Be the change that you want to see first and then let your actions be your message. Wordless sermons often carry the biggest impact. Let your doing be your sermon.

One of my favorite authors is Charles Dickens, creator of the well-known Christmas villain, the penny-pinching miser Scrooge. Who else but Scrooge demonstrates the transformation possible due to personal reflection followed by immediate action? Make it your mission to transform parts of you that are not to your liking. Start on interior flaws first, and the outer self will shape up soon enough.

Serving Others Will Help You

Dr. Napoleon Hill

One of the surest ways to achieve your own success in life is by helping others to attain theirs. Almost anyone can contribute money toward those less fortunate. But the truly affluent person is the one who can afford to give of himself, of his time and energy, to the benefit of others. In so doing he enriches himself beyond measure.

John Wanamaker, the Philadelphia merchant king, once said that the most profitable habit was that of "rendering useful service where it is not expected." And Edward Bok, the great editor of *Ladies Home Journal*, said he rose from poverty to wealth through the practice of "making myself useful to others without regard to what I received in return."

Helping Takes Effort

It takes a conscious effort to give your time and energy to others. You can't simply say, "All right, I'm willing to help anyone who needs my help." You must make a creative project of rendering service to your fellow man.

Perhaps some down-to-earth examples will help you think of ways you can win friends by helping others. There was, for instance, a merchant in an eastern city who built a successful business through a very simple process. Every hour or so one of his clerks checked the parking meters near the store.

Pennies Win Friends

When the clerk spotted an "expired" sign, he dropped a penny in the slot, and attached a note to the car telling the owner that the merchant was pleased to protect him against the inconvenience of a traffic ticket. Many motorists dropped in to thank the merchant—and remained to buy. The owner of a big Boston men's store inserts a neatly printed card in the pocket of each suit he sells, It tells the purchaser that if he finds the suit satisfactory, he may bring the card back after six months and exchange it for any necktie he chooses. Naturally, the buyer always comes back pleased with the suit—and is a ripe prospect for another sale.

The highest paid woman employee of the Bankers Trust Co. in New York City got her start by offering to work three months without pay in order to demonstrate her executive ability. And Butler Stork gave of himself so freely as a prisoner in the Ohio State Penitentiary that he was released, beating a 20-year sentence for forgery. Stork organized a correspondence school that taught more than 1,000 inmates a variety of courses without charge to them or the state. He even induced the International Correspondence School to donate textbooks. The plan attracted so much attention that Stork was given his freedom as a reward.

Put Your Own Mind to Work

Assess your own ability and energy. Who needs your help? How can you help them? It doesn't take money. All it takes is ingenuity and a strong desire to be of genuine service. Helping others solve their problems will help you solve your own.

Think and Grow Rich Newsletter. September, 1993, p. 4.

Chapter 49

While we may not understand why things happen the way they do when they happen, with time and patience and understanding and above all—with faith—we come to learn that everything happens for a reason, in its proper place and time. "Time is relentless in preserving the seed of an equivalent benefit that hides within a defeat," says Dr. Hill. "The best time to begin looking for that seed in a new defeat is now."

—Santa Claus

In prayer, what we desire most often doesn't show up in our lives. When we pray for specific things, we can become dismayed when they don't arrive on schedule. It could very well be that another plan is at work for our higher good. By praying for a particular outcome, we are limiting the gifts we are willing to receive. For example, a child who receives a book instead of the newest version of a video game can be visibly disappointed. If truth be known, the book could be the better tool for later positive outcomes in life. When we are open to what the Universe can provide, we are thinking expansively. When we dictate what we will accept, we are unintentionally diminishing our potential results.

The power of prayer works in conjunction with the words that we choose to make our appeal to the Higher Power. In this season of giving and receiving, many of us prepare "wish lists" that detail what we are willing to accept. It is not just any video game, phone, or DVD, but only a specific one that will meet our qualifications. Disappointment can occur when something other than the designated gift is received.

Could it be time to ask ourselves why the quality of the gift is more important than the act of giving? The best intention of the giver can be ruined when our expectation doesn't coincide with the gift. Avoid the disappointment by being willing to accept what comes your way in the spirit of a greater good at work.

In writing about Cosmic Habitforce, Dr. Hill states:

Strange and imponderable, indeed, are the powers of the human mind. The only provable fact one may know concerning the power of the mind is that each individual mind is but a tiny projection of Infinite Intelligence, whose source is the great reservoir of Intelligence that keeps the stars and planets afloat in space, in their accustomed places, and binds together the infinitesimal portions of the atoms of matter. Yes, and one other important fact, that this mind-power may be shaped into any pattern the individual projector of it desires, with assurance that this pattern will duplicate itself in material form, through the most practical available sources, provided only that the pattern is definite and is held continuously in the spotlight of enduring faith.

Dr. Hill assures us that what we hold in thought, sooner or later will be delivered on our doorstep just as surely as Santa makes his yearly visit on Christmas Eve. Carefully consider what you ask for this year, because you may just receive it. Look to the Higher Good, and put yourself in the universal flow. You may just enjoy the ride!

Opportunity

Dr. Napoleon Hill

Never in the history of the world has opportunity been so abundant as it is now.

We have learned that men are limited only by their own lack of self-confidence and faith in their fellowmen.

The way in which Nature has yielded up her secrets to mankind during these past twenty years has proved that we can accomplish much when we learn to expect much of ourselves.

We have been taught the folly of strife and revenge and the virtue of co-operative effort. The world war taught us that the winner is also the loser when men engage in any sort of destructive effort.

With all these great lessons which we have learned we stand face to face, now, with the opportunity to impose the sum total of what we have learned upon the minds of our children so that it may become a part of their philosophy and lead the next generation to heights of attainment that will startle the world.

This is the only method through which we can pass on to posterity the benefit of that which we have learned through combat, struggle and experimentation. What a glorious opportunity now awaits the leadership of men and women in the Schools, Churches and the Public Press, the three leading mediums through which these great lessons can be firmly planted in the minds of our young.

Those who see this opportunity and have the initiative and the courage to embrace it may sweep on to fame and fortune on the wings of a powerful force that has arisen out of the agitation, strife and chaos of the past seven years.

Let us all contribute our individual support and co-operation to the end that our children may be taught the advantages of placing principle above the dollar and humanity, as a whole, above the individual.

Napoleon Hill's Magazine. January, 1922, Vol. 1, No. 8.

Chapter 50

Keep focused on your goals, do the right thing, and don't waste your time trying to please or live up the expectations of others who, when the chips are down, will do nothing for you.

—Elie Alperstein

In keeping with the tradition of taking inventory of what lessons have been learned during the past year, I would like to offer you my year-end thoughts.

First: Know that the sun rises every single day even after the darkest night. Decide to be there to watch the sunrise.

Second: Remember that the Creator is benevolent. Look to this day for all the gifts brought to you that are seldom acknowledged. An exquisite flower, a crisp breeze, a star twinkling in the midnight blue sky, the scent of a pine tree, a purring senior cat, a bonfire to gather around, fresh sheets and pillowcases, water to refresh, and the ability to look and appreciate all the extraordinary beauty the world has to offer.

Third: Be in the moment. Stay in the moment, moment by moment. The present is all we have. Longing for the past and worrying about the future are fruitless endeavors.

Fourth: Cherish hellos and goodbyes. Neither is long enough, so make the most of each one.

Fifth: Welcome change even if it's an uninvited guest. Know that you could be entertaining "angels" unaware. Change is the one constant. Make friends with it.

Sixth: Embrace the real you. There is no one else like you in the Universe. You are truly one of a kind and put here for a higher purpose.

Seventh: Learn to love the mundane task. By polishing your skills through repetition, repetition, repetition you will shine with the stars.

Eighth: Allow others to speak and you simply listen. This is a good exercise in self-control and personal development.

Ninth: Accept the inevitable because it always is.

Tenth: Express gratitude daily for the acquaintances, friends, and loved ones the Universe has gifted you with in your life. These are your true priceless treasures.

Eleventh: Memorize the following statement: "Let nothing disturb you. Let nothing frighten you. All things are changing. God alone is changeless. Patience attains the good." –St. Teresa of Avila.

And, a good thought to follow every day by Henry Drummond states:

I shall pass through this world but once. Any good therefore, that I can do, or any kindness that I can show to any human being, let me do it now. Let me not deter or neglect it, for I shall not pass this way again.

What Nineteen Hundred and Twenty-One Has Taught Me

Dr. Napoleon Hill

Once a year we should take a retrospective view of life to see what useful knowledge we have gathered.

In my inventory of the past year's experiences I find much to guide me in the future. Among other lessons which Nineteen Hundred and Twenty-one has taught me are the following:

First: That it pays to perform more service and better service than one is paid to perform.

Second: That the destroyer is, in turn, destroyed, usually by the reaction of his own destructive efforts.

Third: That Time is the friend of the man who is right and the enemy of the man who is wrong at heart, no matter how clever he may be in the art of deception.

Fourth: That every effect has a cause, and, that the effect corresponds, in nature, to the cause.

Fifth: That like attracts like; that one can no more saturate his mind with thoughts of selfishness, fear and failure and still succeed than he could sow thistles and reap clover.

Sixth: That the Golden Rule is more powerful than the Rule of Gold.

Seventh: That happiness comes only from helping others find it.

I approach my work for the coming year with renewed faith in the philosophy of the foregoing seven paragraphs, and, with positive evidence that I will get out of life exactly in proportion to what I put into it.

Napoleon Hill's Magazine. January, 1922, Vol. 1, No. 8.

CHAPTER 51

*When I think about growing older and facing illness, I realize
that who I am has nothing to do with how old or healthy this body
is or even this body at all. Who I am goes on into eternity.*

—Karen Larsen

As we begin a new year many of us reflect on housecleaning—both in our external (physical) and internal (spiritual) homes. Cleaning clutter always takes a toll because of the emotional attachment that is so easily attributed to things that hold memories for us. Sometimes, it is easy to release items and memories from our collection once their usefulness is complete, and other times it is traumatic. How can we ease this process so that clutter doesn't control our lives?

Perhaps by looking for the "rightful" owner of the item in the here and now, we can find a useful home for things that currently are taking up precious space. A few years ago a friend of mine moved home to Italy, and she had to dispense of many items in her existing household. She was determined to find homes for her treasures because she literally could not take them with her as she relocated.

She would ask the following question to friends and co-workers: "Does this item belong to you?" She was not inquiring as to whether or not a person lost or misplaced this item, but whether it had a purpose in their current life. If it did, she would give the item to the person. And, to this day, I remember her generosity when I use items that she gave to me. The scent of the flower truly stays on the hand of the giver!

Why not ask yourself what items you currently own that can be "gifted" to someone else for immediate use? Are you hanging on to seldom worn clothing, used books, holiday items, furniture, or children's playthings? Make a point to weekly find a home for some of these things so that you can release the blocked energy in your home. You will feel better for the breathing space that you create in both your outer and inner worlds. Then, take time to smell the flowers!

Living Your Own Life May Take Some "House Cleaning"

Dr. Napoleon Hill

By the time we reach adulthood, most of us have acquired a good deal of clutter in our lives. As you begin to know yourself and know the image of the life you want to build, you will recognize this clutter. Throw it out!

You might begin by discarding some of those acquaintances who waste your time, interfere with your efforts and try to manage you. Clear them out! You need not turn them into enemies, but when you want to be yourself you will find ways to avoid any person who tries to deny you the inalienable right of being yourself.

There is also the self-made clutter which results from not having a clear idea of how you wish to use each day. Make up a time budget. Allot your time in favor of the "musts" which apply to anyone who wants to live his own life profitably and pleasantly.

Eight hours a day is a good allotment for sleep and for rest.

Eight hours a day is a good allotment for work at your business or profession; but as your pattern of life-success grows stronger, probably your hours of work will grow less.

The remaining eight hours are particularly precious. You should divide them into various periods, each of which will be devoted to something you wish to do, not something you have to do. What do you wish to do? Stop now and think. Make a list, such as:

Play, Social Life, Reading, Writing, Playing a Musical Instrument, Extending Your Knowledge in some field that has nothing to do with your making a living, Tending Your Garden, Building Gadgets in Your Home Workshop, Hiking, Boating, and "Just Sitting" and watching the clouds or the stars...

I repeat, those remaining eight hours are particularly precious. They are YOUR FREE TIME in which you may live your own life precisely as you wish to live it. You may find this takes some courage. You may have acquired an exaggerated sense of duty toward others (often a pretty description for plain meddling). You may too well remember being told in childhood such nonsense as "the devil finds work for idle hands." But then, it takes courage to be one's self and avoid the pressures to be like other people and let them live your life for you.

Grow Rich With Peace of Mind. Fawcett, 1995, pp. 129–130.

CHAPTER 52

I challenge you, for the next seven days, to answer, "Amazing!"
every time someone asks you how you are doing. Notice the reac-
tion you get. Notice how it makes you feel. Be prepared for the
conversations it will start.

— Tom Cunningham

J ust as food coloring can make a dish more appetizing or less
appealing, our choice of words can color our world. Thinking
positively requires a student of success to practice using words that
have positive connotations. Whether we feel it is a beautiful day outside
or not, by saying so we condition our minds to find the beauty in the
moment. Lamenting the bad weather, cursing the cold, using terminology that intimidates, all make our world a less inviting place. Have you
ever looked at a single flower and found it to be absolutely exquisite
only to hear someone else complain that it wasn't a full blown bouquet?
Or, have you ever gone to the beach and witnessed a striking sunset
that could have been a Van Gogh, Renoir, or Monet painting (your
choice) only to have someone look down at this moment of splendour
and decry the smelly fish washed up on the beach? Beauty is definitely
where you find it.

Neutral words do not impact us. They do not position us in one
direction or another. They leave us smack in the middle of wherever
we find ourselves. Positive word choices, however, help us become
winners. They ease our way into a home run, completing a marathon,
and becoming the best version of ourselves we choose to be.

When you use positive self-talk, you are giving yourself a spiritual
massage. It feels good, and it can produce good results as long as you
work toward achieving the expectations that you set for yourself. Don't

fool yourself in believing that you are someone or something you are not. Rather accept the challenge of giving yourself positive self-talk daily—even hourly—to heighten your awareness of what you can become one positive affirmation at a time. Truly, when you believe it you will be it!

Habits of Thought

Dr. Napoleon Hill

The drifter makes no attempt to discipline or control his thoughts, and he never learns the difference between positive thinking and negative thinking. He allows his mind to drift with any stray thought which may float into it. People who drift in connection with their thought habits are sure to drift on other subjects as well.

In an allegorical account of an interview with the devil it was stated that the devil said he feared nothing except that the world might sometime produce a thinker who would use his own mind, adding significantly that he controlled all drifters who neglected to use their own minds. The devil is not the only individual who exploits the drifter. And the drifter is the victim not only of all those who wish to exploit him, but he is also the victim of all the stray, negative thoughts which park themselves in his mind.

The non-drifter takes full possession of his own mind through self-discipline, and organizes definite plans and purposes. He directs his mind to whatever ends he desires, and he keeps his mind occupied with the things he wants and off the things he does not want.

A positive mental attitude is the first and the most important of the twelve riches of life, and it cannot be attained by the drifter. It can be attained only by a scrupulous regard for time, through habits of self-discipline. No amount of time devoted to one's occupation can compensate for the benefits of a positive mental attitude, for this is the power which makes the use of time effective and productive.

A positive mental attitude does not grow voluntarily, like the weeds of the fields. It requires cultivation, through carefully disciplined habits of thought. And the greatest of all training grounds for the cultivation of a positive mental attitude is provided by one's chosen occupation, where he spends the greatest part of his life. Here you may combine your efforts to make them financially productive and to develop a positive mental attitude.

When you get your own thought habits under control, you will have yourself under control, but you cannot do it by drifting. Organize your thoughts. Decide what you want, to what position in life you aspire. Then plan ways and means to express your thoughts in terms of organized action. Follow through with applied faith and unremitting persistence. This is the means by which you can become the master of your fate, the captain of your soul.

Waste no time worrying about what others may think. The important thing is what you think and do.

PMA Science of Success. Pp. 463–464.

"WHATEVER THE MIND CAN CONCEIVE AND BELIEVE, THE MIND CAN ACHIEVE."

Napoleon Hill

For more information about Napoleon Hill products, please contact the following:

The Napoleon Hill Foundation
University of Virginia–Wise
College Relations Apt. C
1 College Avenue
Wise, Virginia 24293

Don Green, Executive Director
Annedia Sturgill, Executive Assistant

Telephone: 276.328.6700
Email: napoleonhill@uvawise.edu

Website: www.naphill.org

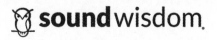